tyranny |ˈtirənē|

noun (pl. tyrannies)

cruel and oppressive government or rule: *people who survive war and escape tyranny* | *the removal of the regime may be the end of a tyranny.*

• a nation under such cruel and oppressive government.

• cruel, unreasonable, or arbitrary use of power or control: *she resented his rages and his tyranny* | figurative : *the tyranny of the nine-to-five day* | *his father's tyrannies.*

• (especially in ancient Greece) rule by one who has absolute power without legal right.

New Oxford English Dictionary, 3rd Edition

 IN THIS ISSUE

LA+ TYRANNY
EDITORIAL

From the first utopian impulse of Plato's Republic to today's global border controls and public space surveillance systems, there has always been a tyrannical aspect to the organization of society and the regulation of its spaces. Tyranny takes many forms, from the rigid barriers of military zones to the subtle ways in which landscape is used to 'naturalize' power. What are these forms and how do they function at different scales, in different cultures, and at different times in history? How are designers and other disciplines complicit in the manifestation of these varying forms of tyranny and how have they been able to subvert such political and ideological structures? These are the issues that concern us in this edition of LA+.

We begin our exploration of the theme with Steve Basson's opening historical survey of the role of public squares in both the expression of freedom and the manifestation of tyranny. Basson reminds us just how important design of public space can be to cultural and political engagement in a city. Historian Chang-tai Hung examines the specific example of Beijing's Tiananmen Square, explaining how it has served as a theatrical stage for the political agenda of the Chinese Communist Party since 1949. Of course, no one can forget the events of June 1989 when student protesters in Tiananmen were forcibly suppressed by government troops, but it is the events that unfolded during the 2011–2012 'Arab Spring' and subsequent global protests of the Occupy movement that have truly revealed just how crucial the increasingly designed public spaces of the neoliberal city have become to the politics of citizen resistance. In this vein, Egyptian sociologist Mona Abaza highlights how the ever-changing graffiti in a particular street in Cairo became emblematic of the revolutionary protests during the Arab Spring, while geographer and political theorist Erik Swyngedouw takes stock of this groundswell of discontent. Swyngedouw's description of contemporary activists as "insurgent architects" is reinforced by Stephen Graham who sets out a range of methods by which words and images have been used by activists and artists to subvert and disrupt what he refers to as the "new military urbanism." Fionn Byrne extends this military metaphor, drawing historical connections between landscape architecture and military technology and logistics.

Rooted in Marxist critiques of the neoliberal city, Swyngedouw and Graham are not recalling a utopia of the proletariat; rather, they are trying to articulate what a genuinely democratic city could be. Coming at the same problem from a different angle is architect Chris Marcinkoski, whose research locates and scrutinizes the development front of speculative global capital. Marcinkoski argues that designers are complicit in destructive 'boom and bust' development cycles and that they need to foster new techniques to direct these forces toward more socially and ecologically responsible ends.

But the geography of tyranny is not always as clear-cut as the defined urban spaces of protest suggest. With Rodrigo Firmino as our guide we trace tyranny's digital coding, examining the rise of technological surveillance in urban Brazil and its impact on public space, while with Matthew Gandy we consider how artificial light–used to enhance safety, security, and production–now engenders a new form of tyranny through excessive light pollution, which risks damaging both our circadian rhythms and our environment. Scanning tyranny's deceptive horizons, Casey Brown examines the creation of "stateless space" in border zones designed to deter would-be immigrants and asylum seekers, and we reach tyranny's demoralizing and banal endpoint in a refugee camp in northern Iraq, the design of which is unpacked and critiqued by Jim Kennedy. These disparate territories are punctuated and extended by the LA+ team in graphic spreads that reach from Saddam Hussein's former pleasure grounds on the banks of the Tigris to the specious creation of new sovereign land in the South China Sea.

Also in this issue, artists Jesse Krimes and Hasan Elahi explore tyranny's psychological depths, respectively finding beauty and sardonic humor in different forms of incarceration. These individual heterotopias are amplified in collective sites of commemoration such as New York City's 9/11 memorial, which semiotician Patrizia Violi reviews, and a very different form of memorial in Rwanda, where Nick Pevzner explains that *umuvumu* trees now stand as an eerie reminder of the Tutsi homesteads erased during that country's genocide. And finally, in the provocative closing essay of this issue, Richard Weller exposes the tyranny of the view, marking how designs of urban public space are invariably represented as Photoshopped versions of an "eco-paradise." As Weller notes, landscape architects can't avoid the political tensions of contemporary culture by hiding behind images of nature as if both it and they were merely innocent bystanders.

Tatum L. Hands
Editor in Chief

STEVE BASSON

BLOOD. ON

THE SQUARE

Steve Basson is Associate Professor of Architectural History and Theory at the School of Built Environment, Curtin University, Perth, Australia. His current research is concerned with historiographical and epistemological questions that focus on re-evaluating conventional approaches to architectural and urban history, especially in relation to how public space is understood from the perspective and context of the past.

✚ HISTORY, URBAN DESIGN, CULTURAL STUDIES

In a speech delivered to the National Convention on February 5, 1794, Maximilien Robespierre declared the Terror as the primary means to defeat the enemies of the French Republic, given that the "terror is nothing else than justice, prompt, secure and inflexible."[1] As a strategy of government, Robespierre went on to describe the Terror as both an emanation of virtue and a consequence of democracy's general principles. However, it was in the Place de la Concorde (then known as Place de la Revolution) that the reality of the Terror could be found actively at work through the instrument of the guillotine and mass execution of citizens. A month earlier, this same square had played host to the execution of Louis XVI before citizens and upwards of 80,000 National Guard and police.[2] What the Place de la Concorde represented here was a site dedicated to the repression of a population and the public spectacle of dispatching any who would speak out or demonstrate against the orthodoxy of the republican revolution. It was also here, between September 1793 and July 1794, that free speech and protest were eradicated within a setting that extolled the virtues of the guillotine as a tool of social and political tyranny.

This picture of tyranny associated with the Place de la Concorde is not how public squares are usually perceived. On the contrary, public squares are historically portrayed as necessary and timeless settings for the practice and defense of free political debate and protest. This is a history that takes us back to the ancient Greek square, the *agora*, which, according to Hannah Arendt, celebrated the higher and civilized attributes of the human condition through the free pursuits of political and cultural activity. In particular, Arendt saw the *agora* as defining a specific locus of political organization that brought into being free action and speech as the constituent parts of each citizen's political life.[3] Paul Zucker also saw the genuine first appearance of an *agora* in ancient Greece as an outcome of democracy and the need for a space to serve the political practices of an assembled citizenry.[4] Charles Jenks and Maggie Valentine follow this when saying that the Greek development of the *agora* as an "outdoor room, or open assembly space, remains to this day the primary expression of, and allowance for, democracy, since without it the public cannot feel its strength and make up its collective mind."[5]

It is from such a background that the public square as a privileged urban and architectural formation is still perceived to represent a site fundamental to the continued expression and practice of freedom. And why not? Certainly such spaces have been at the epicenter of numerous struggles against corruption, discrimination, or despotism. The public squares of the USA were filled with voices calling for equality and emancipation during the struggle for African-American civil rights and again during protests against the Vietnam War. Tiananmen Square would later symbolize the pure power of such space when unified with a people's profound call for freedom and change. The more recent revolutions that marked the 2011 Arab Spring were largely centered on mass demonstrations that took place in the main squares of cities such as Tunis, Cairo, Alexandria, and Benghazi.[6] The same year also saw the Occupy Movement begin its global protests against social and economic inequality, again centered in public squares.[7] Such events reinforce an intimate relationship between public squares and the voice and purpose of liberty and democracy. These same events also suggest a clear connection between the design of public squares and their impact upon behavior via a space that preserves and promotes the singular ends of free speech and action in service of the greater human good. It is, then, as a site of heroic protest that we have come to understand such spaces as synonymous with the collective will of a people focused on equality, justice, and freedom; with righting the wrongs of government and institutions; and where one can still expect to hear, as in ages past, the passionate and collective cry of *'liberté ou la morte.'*

Another History

But, as mentioned earlier, public squares are not urban or architectural creations specific to the enactment of democracy and free speech alone. Such a view can only exist within an edited version of history that supports what is desirable rather than what has always been there. Tyranny has also comprised an active part of the life of public squares, as captured by George Orwell through a chilling picture of this other history in his novel *Nineteen Eighty-Four*. In the dystopian world Orwell created, the public squares of London were employed as sites of systemic execution; propaganda and anti-Semitism; and processions, speeches and singing in praise of Big Brother. In Orwell's fictional Victory Square—once Trafalgar Square—Big Brother replaced the statue of Lord Nelson, whilst its social and political practices, as well as architectural and spatial narratives, transferred to the truth and virtues of "IngSoc" and the doctrine that war is peace, freedom is slavery, and ignorance is strength.[8] In this square, as in all others, citizens were always in the view of cameras and the silent presence of thought police.

Nineteen Eighty-Four is filled with echoes of the darker events that have, throughout history, inhabited public squares. The early years of Germany's Nazi regime saw public squares across Hitler's Reich decked out in swastika banners; hosting celebrations and festivals in honor of Nazi political, racial, and cultural supremacy; and subjected to temporary or more permanent architectural modifications such as the Nazi Honor Temples in Munich's Konigsplatz or the Nazi pylon erected in the south square of the Herrengasse in Graz, Austria.[9] During the 1930s and later, propaganda, exhibitions of military might, and parades also graced the public squares of the Soviet Union, most impressively in Moscow's Red Square. And today, Kim Il-sung Square in Pyongyang, North Korea, serves as a site equally for militaristic demonstrations and pageants in praise of yet another despotic regime.[10]

It is from an equally selective reading that Tiananmen Square is claimed as a triumph for the righteous cause of liberty. Left out of this narrative is that this same space in 1989 hosted a victory

1 Maximilien Marie Isidore de Robespierre, "Terror is Nothing Else Than Justice," in Brian MacArthur [ed] *The Penguin Book of Historic Speeches* [Harmondsworth: Penguin, 1996], 184.

2 Antoine De Baecque, *Glory and the Terror: Seven Deaths Under the French Revolution* [New York: Routledge, 2001], 94.

3 Hannah Arendt, *The Human Condition* [Chicago: Chicago University Press, 1958].

4 Paul Zucker, *Town and Square* [Cambridge Mass: MIT Press, 1970].

5 Charles Jenks & Maggie Valentine, "The Architecture of Democracy: The Hidden Tradition," *Architectural Design* 57, no. 9–10 [1987]: 10.

6 Nasser Rabbat, "The Arab Revolution Takes Back th Preface to Occupy: Three Inquiries in Disobedience," *Critical Enquiry* 39, no. 1 [2012]: 1–7.

7 George Orwell, *Nineteen Eighty-Four* [London: Heinemann, 1965].

9 Joshua Hagen, "Parades, Public Space, and Propaganda: The Nazi Culture Parades in Munich," *Geografiska Annaler, Series B. Human Geography* 90, no. 4 [2008]: 349-367; Hans Haake, "Und ihr habt gesiegt 1988," *October* 48, Spring [1989]: 79–87.

10 Iurii Gerchuk, "Festival Decoration of the City: The Materialization of the Communist Myth in the 1930s," *Journal of Design History* 13, no. 2 [2000]: 123–136; Suk-Young Kim, "Springtime for Kim Il-sung in Pyongyang: City On Stage, City as Stage," *TDR* 51, no. 2 [2007]: 24–40.

Zucotti Park, New York City

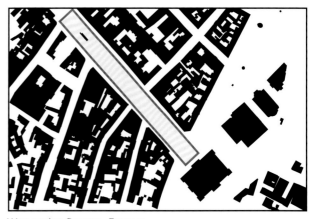

Wenceslas Square, Prague

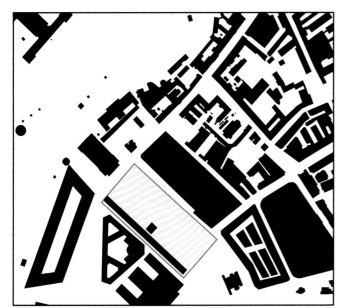

Red Square, Moscow

Syntagma Square, Athens

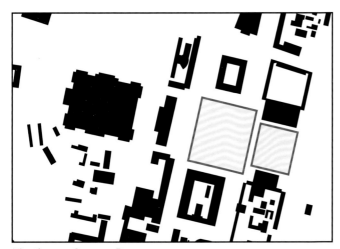

Kim Il-sung Square, Pyongyang

Independence Square, Ukraine

Place de la Concorde, Paris

Taksim Square, Istanbul

Königsplatz, Munich

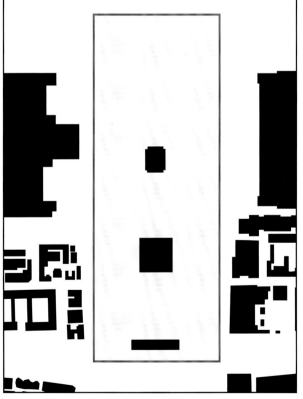

Tiananmen Square, Beijing

500'

for the authoritarian military forces sent in to crush this brief call for freedom. The design of squares assists the pageantry and propaganda of tyranny along with the ease of troop and tank deployments as also witnessed during the 1956 uprising in Hungary and in 1968's 'Prague Spring' in Czechoslovakia. Tahrir Square (or Liberation Square) in Cairo has been feted as a site of freedom since the protests that began the movement known as the 2011 Arab Spring. And yet the democratically elected government and head of state that emerged from this revolution were in 2013 brought down by mass protests that again centered on Tahrir Square. This counter-revolution of 2013 also returned to power the same authoritarian regime that had been ousted by the original 2011 uprisings.[11]

The *vox populi* associated with public squares does not always stand for justice, virtue, or democracy. Squares provide a platform for protests that call for genuine reform and emancipation, or for prejudice and denial of rights. In 1780, the public squares and streets of London were filled with protests and violent demonstrations against the Roman Catholic Relief Act of 1778. Spurred on by Lord George Gordon and the Protestant Association, 60,000 protesters sought to pressure the government to repeal a law that afforded rights and emancipation for Roman Catholics in Britain. It was in the name of denying freedom and upholding intolerance that the Gordon Riots saw buildings and prisons burnt down, 285 people killed and 25 protestors hung.[12]

Hate, intolerance, and prejudice can act as powerful tools of tyranny, as can the tactics of hidden arrests and the use of surveillance technologies. Public squares are no stranger to either of these. It was in the middle of the night that the New York Police sought to evict members of the Occupy movement from Zuccotti Park whilst also "forcibly preventing journalists and cameras from recording the tactics of the police."[13] But while police actions such as these are of concern, state and corporate surveillance systems via CCTV, facial recognition programs, and data interception and retention capabilities, cast an equally ominous shadow across the surface of public squares. Systems such as these were designed to combat and deter crime and terrorism. But between Bentham's Panopticon, Orwell's Big Brother state, and the revelations of Edward Snowden, more questions are raised than answered by the sheer scale, depth, and reach of contemporary surveillance technologies.[14] All major public squares today are electronically monitored. And yet beyond the stated goals of such systems lies a vast potential that governments are reticent to disclose in terms of what information or identities are collected and for what purposes. As Hille Koskela says: "The question here is not about 'crime control' but rather about 'control' in a wider sense."[15] In short, this is a question of power: who wields it, and who is subjected to it. But for public squares and those who inhabit them, especially in the cause of free speech and protest, it is also a question of losing anonymity. Kevin Haggerty and Richard Ericson referred to this as the ultimate outcome of what they described as the "surveillant assemblage"

and "the disappearance of disappearance."[16] And yet, given Arendt's conception of public squares as a space of necessary appearance, perhaps in the age of the surveillance state, public squares have instead transposed into an urban form centered on the appearance of appearance.

Contested Terrains

We have inherited a past that speaks to the exceptionalism of public squares as sites especial to benign, emancipatory, and democratic practices. But this is a past that is built on what Michel Foucault referred to as subjugated knowledge, where historical contents have been buried or masked in order to preserve the privileged nature of a particular narrative.[17] Public spaces instead define a mode of space that is equally accommodating to strategies of propaganda, surveillance, and repression; of collective voices raised in support of intolerance, racism, and authoritarian ideologies; and of death via executions, the mob, or the military. The practice of capital punishment, of course, is not exclusive to totalitarian regimes and comprises another largely unrecognized history of the public square.[18] Nevertheless, while individuals such as Colin Rowe and Fred Koetter speak of the destruction of the traditional city, or Michael Sorkin of the privatization of the city, as reasons for the demise of public space, such positions inevitably rely on some prior condition of pure public space or that anything repressive by definition is alien to such space.[19] The reality is that terror and tyranny comprise an integral and historically recurrent feature of public squares. After Caesar crossed the Rubicon, he then placed troops loyal only to him within the forums of Rome. Through such acts, a republic was transformed into a dictatorship.

The public square is, then, a stage upon which the socio-political conditions and rationalities of any given period are acted out. As such, it marks out a contextual terrain of contested truths, values, and realities. Here there is nothing continuous or essentialist, only contingent. It would also be problematic to assume that when acting as a site for Robespierre's Terror, Soviet oppression, or Nazi torchlight parades, those involved were sadistic or psychopathic. As Stanley Milgram observed, "ordinary people, simply doing their jobs, and without any particular hostility on their part, can become agents in a terrible destructive process."[20] Such is the persuasive power of obedience to authority; conformity and belief in the rationalization of particular cultural, social, or political ideologies; and of course, the banality of evil. To understand the public square is to recognize it as a site that concentrates and amplifies what can be seen, said, or acted upon at a particular time.

The reading of public squares that emerges from this is very different from traditional narratives based on the classical ideal of the *agora*. It also erodes any direct connection between social activities and the urban and architectural elements that compose the physical landscape of public squares. Certainly, if the form of public squares and the buildings that frame them remain the same while the practices within them exist in a state of transition and contradiction, this would question the automatic presumption that design can impact positively upon the behavior of occupants. During the 19th century, Union Square in New York became a traditional site for mass meetings and protests, especially in relation to the labor movement. Whilst not designed for such activity, in 1873 the north end of the square was specifically adapted to accommodate mass meetings and to provide, as Joanna Merwood-Salisbury observed, an "urban space for the sanctioned exercise of democracy."[21] Tolerance for these mass meetings and protests–which at times had become violent– diminished during the early years of the 20th century leading to a redesign in 1931 that sought to eliminate mass meetings from the square. This "attempt to depoliticize Union Square through design" nevertheless failed, it continuing instead to perform as a site of political protest.[22]

When asked whether there was any example of architecture that ensured freedom, Michel Foucault said, "I do not think that there is anything functionally–by its very nature–absolutely liberating," adding later, "the guarantee of freedom is freedom."[23] Further on in the same article, however, he suggested that positive effects might be achieved if the intentions of the architecture coincided "with the real practice of people in the exercise of their freedom."[24] What Foucault spoke to here were the same limits and challenges of design expressed through the example of Union Square. But to take up this challenge would require an approach that, as Malcolm Miles suggests, moves beyond form and incorporates the plurality of events and readings that bring with them new insights such as from geography, sociology, and culture.[25] Such a course would, however, not be simple.

Conclusion

The public square that we have come to know is largely a creation of myth. Yes, protests in the cause of freedom and equality are an active constituent of many such spaces, but so too are the trappings of tyranny. An assembly of citizens can meet in the name of emancipation on one day, while on another promote prejudice and hate. What is just, virtuous, and democratic can encompass a struggle for civil rights or the grim and menacing figure of the guillotine. The public square represents a contested terrain of radically contrasting histories, politics, and meanings. Against this, our understanding and design of such spaces cannot operate in a vacuum or treat form as a primary and functional condition of behavioral modification. What this demands is the employment of social, cultural, and political relationships to inform knowledge and design processes; to identify actual and active rather than imagined sites engaged in the practice of democratic debate and human rights; and to define strategies that facilitate as opposed to presumptions that design on its own is enough. Such is the challenge. But then such has ever been the challenge of freedom against the various and real forces of tyranny.

11 Robert Fisk, "When is a Military coup not a military coup? When it Happens in Egypt, Apparently," *The Independent Newspaper* (July 4, 2013), http://www.independent.co.uk/voices/comment/when-is-a-military-coup-not-a-military-coup-when-it-happens-in-egypt-apparently-8688000.html.

12 George F.E. Rude, "The Gordon Riots: A Study of the Rioters and Their Victims," *Transactions of the Royal Historical Society* 6, (1956): 93–114.

13 W.J.T. Mitchell, "Preface to Occupy," 6.

14 Michel Foucault, *Discipline and Punish: The Birth of the Prison* (trans. A Sheridan) (Harmondsworth: Penguin, 1991); Julian Sanchez, "Snowden showed us just how big the Panopticon really was: now it is up to us," *The Guardian Newspaper* (June 5, 2014), http://www.theguardian.com/commentisfree/2014/jun/05/edward-snowden-one-year-surveillance-debate-begins-future-privacy (accessed April 28, 2015).

15 Hille Koskela, "The Gaze without Eyes: Video-surveillance and the changing nature of urban space," *Progress in Human Geography* 24, no. 2 (2000): 260.

16 Kevin D. Haggerty & Richard V. Ericson, "The Surveillant Assemblage," *British Journal of Sociology* 51, no. 4 (2000): 605–22.

17 Michel Foucault, *Society Must Be Defended: Lectures at the College De France 1975–1976* (New York: Picador, 2003), 7–9.

18 Steve Basson, "Oh Comrade What Times Those Were! History, Capital Punishment and the Urban Square," *Urban Studies* 43, no. 7 (2006): 1147–58.

19 Colin Rowe & Fred Koetter, *Collage City* (Cambridge, Mass: MIT Press, 1976); Michael Sorkin, *Variations on a Theme Park: The New American City and the End of Public Space* (New York: Hill and Wang, 1992).

20 Stanley Milgram, *Obedience to Authority* (New York: Perennial Classics, 2004), 6.

21 Joanna Merwood-Salisbury, "Patriotism and Protest: Union Square as Public Space, 1832–1932," *Journal of the Society of Architectural Historians* 68, no. 4 (2009): 548.

22 Ibid., 555.

23 Michel Foucault, "Space, Knowledge, and Power," in Paul Rabinow (ed) *The Foucault Reader: An introduction to Foucault's Thought* (Harmondsworth: Penguin, 1991), 245.

24 Ibid., 246.

25 Malcolm Miles, "After the Public Realm: Spaces of Representation, Transition and Plurality," *JADE* 19, no. 3 (2000): 253–61.

THE GLARE OF MODERNITY

MATTHEW GANDY

Matthew Gandy is Professor of Geography at Cambridge University. He has published widely on cultural, urban, and environmental themes and his books include *Concrete and Clay: Reworking Nature in New York City* (2004) and *The Fabric of Space: Water, Modernity, and the Urban Imagination* (2015). He is currently writing a book about cultural and scientific aspects to urban biodiversity.

+ GEOGRAPHY, HISTORY

The introduction of artificial light forms a distinctive element in the transformation of urban space under modernity. The replacement of scattered and dimly glowing oil lamps with brighter and denser rows of gas lights during the 19th century, and then new forms of much more effective electric lighting introduced from the late 19th century onwards, forms part of a familiar palimpsest of changes in the urban experience. Artificial light, it seems, is just another facet of modernity that has become little more than a mundane feature of everyday life provoking occasional attention through forms of disruption, display, or the incessant advance of new illuminated surfaces designed to capture our fleeting interest.

Yet the idea of the modern city as an "empire of lights," and its celebration through festivals and illuminated landmarks, obscures a different history of light – where light was exploited as a means of intimidation and control. The gradual introduction of streetlights, for example, cannot be separated from the emergence of modern police forces and their growing presence within the expanding 19th-century metropolis. Historical accounts of lamp smashing in Berlin, Paris, Vienna, and other cities attest to the symbolic significance of these early technologies of surveillance.[1] The presence of urban darkness had an increasingly ambivalent relationship with the modern city since it was perceived as both a source of danger and a form of protection from the prying eyes of the state. There were even fears that better illumination could encourage crime or disorder by making city streets more navigable at night. Although the emergence of street lighting can be placed within the context of the gradual emergence of the liberal subject, and a certain disinterested, routinized, or at least distanciated relationship between society, technology, and the modern state, there is a parallel and more sinister story that extends beyond the more familiar confines of capitalist urbanization and the modernization of urban space in Europe and North America.[2]

The first electric arc lights, introduced in the late 19th century, provoked not only astonishment at their apparent conversion of night into day but also alarm on account of their intense and dazzling glare. So powerful were these lights that entire cities such as Detroit and San Jose sought to provide a system of complete illumination from a small number of lamps installed on high metal towers to provide the imposing spectacle of tower lighting. For contemporary observers such as Robert Louis Stevenson, the arc light was a kind of "urban star" that was "obnoxious to the human eye." "A lamp fit for a nightmare!," wrote Stevenson, "Such a light as this should shine only on murders and public crime, or along the corridors of lunatic asylums, a horror to heighten horror."[3]

The ability of arc lights—later modified as searchlights—to cast a harsh light over a vast area was also harnessed in wartime as a means to terrorize adversaries, especially by European armies engaged in wars of colonial expansionism, as illustrated by the deliberate illumination of the Egyptian port of Alexandria by the British navy in the 1880s. During the First World War, arc lights were also used for the creation of "artificial moonlight" to facilitate attacks by night and they have been widely deployed in naval warfare to dazzle other ships.

Light has also been instrumental to the geopolitical landscapes of the 20th century with ranks of searchlights scouring the night sky or picking out individual human figures seeking a means of escape. Light has become a weapon that can identify targets and eliminate enemies: it can delineate spaces to be destroyed or lurk as a laser in the landscape. The direct use of lasers as weapons has been a focus of interest since the 1980s, especially by the Pentagon in the wake of Ronald Reagan's "star wars" initiative, with the first successful testing of a "directed energy weapon" in the Persian Gulf in 2014 as part of the so-called "zap wars" phase of laser weapon systems under development for the US Navy.[4] Light has also been routinely deployed as a means of torture through sleep deprivation for the victims of extrajudicial rendition held at the Pentagon's global network of "dark sites."[5]

From the 1970s onwards the problem of excessive light has come into sharper focus as a specific problem referred to as light pollution encompassing a range of concerns such as the loss of the night, the disturbance of circadian rhythms, and the wastage of energy. The increase in illumination has also been accompanied by a reduction in human sleep, not just through phenomena such as light trespass that may foster anxiety or insomnia, but also through the role of light in facilitating a 24-hour society of work and consumption. The use of light to extend the working day, initially in 19th-century factories but later spreading to a wider rage of workplaces, has played a role in the production of the "human motor."[6] In his novel *The Rings of Saturn*, for example, W.G. Sebald describes the strange glow of silk-weaving factories at night along with the terrifying machines used to improve human productivity.[7] More recently, the pharmaceutical industry has stepped into the fray to provide the means for artificially regulating diminishing amounts of rest and also helping tired workers to stay awake. The circadian rhythms of the human body have become the focus of cyborgian attempts to reduce the need for "wasteful" corporeal replenishment through sleep.[8] We sleep significantly less than we used to and light forms part of the panoply of digital distractions that seek to replace real dreams with those that have been manufactured for us.

The incessant incandescence of modernity has become even more pervasive in recent decades. Just as arc lights provoked anxiety in the past, the increasingly ubiquitous installation of new, more powerful LED technologies has also provoked disquiet. The world is becoming brighter every year with new satellite images confirming the gradual elimination of darkness and the absorption of the night sky into a murky twilight that extends far beyond cities, industrial installations, and illuminated highways. The perception of lighting systems as a relatively innocuous facet of modernity is being replaced by a multi-faceted set of concerns that extends from the technologies themselves, and their specific emotional or material effects, to the nexus of interests that lie behind these seemingly unstoppable socio-technological entanglements. These new tyrannies of light mark an intensified phase in the inexorable growth of light pollution: light has become an intense focus of concern yet it remains tied into a technological logic that largely eludes political scrutiny. Those few countries such as France and Slovenia that have recently sought to reduce levels of light pollution, and place the question of light in an arena of public contestation, must nonetheless contend with a powerful nexus of interests that are essentially oblivious to a growing range of social, cultural, and ecological concerns. Not for nothing are companies such as Philips, Osram, and GE—which dominate the lighting market—among the most powerful in the world: they have not only sought to aggressively eliminate competition, but also install themselves as part of the malware of modernity.[9] If citizens were to regain control over light it would open up new technological pathways and also reveal political alternatives to the perpetual glare of global capital.

1 Wolfgang Schivelbusch, *Disenchanted Night: The Industrialization of Light in the Nineteenth Century*, trans. A. Davies (Oxford, New York and Hamburg: Berg Publishers, 1988 [1983]).

2 For a rich account of the evolving relationship between light and the liberal subject in the 19th century see Chris Otter, *The Victorian Eye: A Political History of Light and Vision in Britain, 1800–1910* (Chicago: University of Chicago Press, 2008).

3 Cited in Schivelbusch, *Disenchanted Night*, 134.

4 Mark Thompson, "Zap Wars: US Navy Successfully Tests Laser Weapon in the Persian Gulf," *Time* (10 December 2014).

5 Jonathan Crary, *24/7: Late Capitalism and the Ends of Sleep* (London and New York: Verso, 2014).

6 Anson Rabinbach, *The Human Motor: Energy, Fatigue, and the Origins of Modernity* (Berkeley, CA: University of California Press, 1992).

7 W.G. Sebald, *The Rings of Saturn*, trans. Michael Hulse (London: Harvill, 1998 [1995]).

8 See, for example, Crary, *24/7*, and Anson Rabinbach, *The Human Motor*.

9 Examples include the Phoebus Cartel (1924–1939) formed by General Electric, Osram, Philips, Tungsram, and other manufacturers.

CHANG-TAI HUNG

TIANANMEN

THE GRAND POLITICAL THEATER OF THE

SQUARE
CHINESE COMMUNIST PARTY

Chang-tai Hung PhD is Chair Professor Emeritus of Humanities at Hong Kong University of Science and Technology, specializing in modern Chinese cultural history. His publications include *War and Popular Culture: Resistance in Modern China, 1937–1945* (1994) and *Mao's New World: Political Culture in the Early People's Republic* (2011).

✚ HISTORY, POLITICS, URBAN STUDIES

Tiananmen Square, a 44-hectare open space located in the heart of Beijing, is the most controversial political arena in China today. A visit to the square can easily evoke a mixed feeling of wonder and trepidation. On the one hand, visitors' eyes can roam freely over a vast open space – an uninhibited, expanding panorama reaching from Tiananmen Gate in the north to Zhengyang Gate in the south and from the National Museum of China in the east to the Great Hall of the People in the west. This will surely stir pride in many Chinese who see their nation emerging as a world economic power. On the other hand, individuals who are sensitive to their surroundings immediately realize that they are entering one of the world's most closely watched plazas. The area is teeming with policemen and plainclothes public security personnel on the ground, and there are countless surveillance cameras mounted on light poles above. Many visitors perceive that they are being carefully monitored, which engenders a feeling of anxiety and apprehension.

Originally constructed in the 15th century during the Ming dynasty (1368–1644), Tiananmen Square has undergone many transformations over the centuries, from the Qing dynasty (1644–1911) to the Republican era (1912–1949) and the Communist rule (since 1949). It was enlarged to its present immense size in 1959 to commemorate the 10th anniversary of the founding of the People's Republic of China (PRC).[1] It is here that major national events have taken place, including Mao Zedong's declaration of the founding of the PRC on October 1, 1949, and it is here that great spectacles have been staged, the latest being the 60th anniversary celebration of the founding of the PRC in 2009. The square symbolizes and encapsulates the power and supremacy of the ruling Chinese Communist Party (CCP), which claims to represent, and rule in the interests of, the entire Chinese people. Accordingly, Tiananmen Square is commonly dubbed by the official media as "the people's square" (*renmin guangchang*), which means that it epitomizes the voice of the people that the Party heeds in selflessly advancing national interests. In reality, however, the square is not an arena belonging to the people. Instead, it is a political theater monopolized by the CCP to celebrate its communist revolution, rewrite official histories, publicize its marvelous achievements, and exercise tight control over the populace.

Architecture

In the 66 years since 1949, nowhere has the power and domination of the CCP been presented more forcefully than in the domain of Tiananmen Square. The Party dominates this symbolic core of China spatially, historically, and politically, shaping it according to its own image. Architecturally, at the center of the square is the Monument to the People's Heroes, situated along the city's iconic north-south axis – a line stretching eight kilometers from north to south in accordance with the age-old Chinese sacred conception of the royal capital as a perfect geometrical form. Erected in 1958, the monument commemorates those people who sacrificed their lives to save China from Western imperialist aggression and internal wars since the late Qing dynasty. The eight giant reliefs at the obelisk's base embody the CCP's official telling of modern Chinese history: starting from the Opium War of 1839, when China came under aggressive British imperialism, to the victorious conclusion of the Red Army's April 1949 crossing of the Yangzi River to defeat the Nationalist forces in Nanjing, the capital of the Nationalist Party. The Communists here portray themselves as the worthy successors to these selfless men and women who perished while fighting for China's independence, reaffirming one of the most popular propaganda songs of the 1950s, "Without the Chinese Communist Party, There Would Be No New China."

Immediately south of the monument and lying along the same central axial line is the Chairman Mao Memorial Hall, constructed in 1977 to memorialize the late chairman who died a year earlier. In official media, although Mao is partially criticized for his leading role in the tumultuous Cultural Revolution (1966–76) that left the country in ruin, his supreme position in the Party pantheon as leader of the revolution remains secure, at least for now. The current Party leadership, led by General Secretary Xi Jinping, realizes that an all-out campaign to discredit Mao would be tantamount to an attack on the ideological foundation of the entire Party, which would undermine the CCP's legitimacy to rule. Mao's mausoleum, coupled with the chairman's giant portrait hanging on Tiananmen Gate and overlooking the square, speaks clearly that the chairman's ghost is still hovering.

That these two memorials are situated precisely at the center of the square reaffirms their supreme position, overshadowing neighboring structures and confirming the centrality of the CCP in the Chinese psyche. The Party's decision to place not one but two memorials alongside the sacred central axial line is highly problematic and is considered by many Chinese as inauspicious. It also points to an irreconcilable contradiction: while the Communists rebuked China's imperial legacy and traditions as feudal, obsolete, and repressive, they wasted no time in appropriating the ancient hallowed line for their own use.

History

Tiananmen Square is an ideal venue for the Party to tell its own history. The eight reliefs of the Monument to the People's Heroes were designed with that goal in mind. The Party's history is even more systematically and meticulously reconstructed in the National Museum of China,

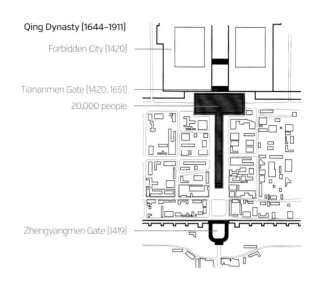

Qing Dynasty (1644–1911)
Forbidden City (1420)
Tiananmen Gate (1420, 1651)
20,000 people
Zhengyangmen Gate (1419)

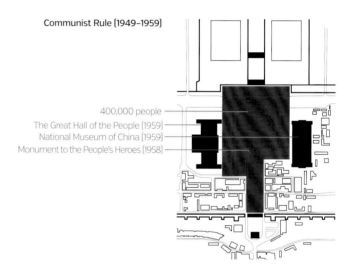

Communist Rule (1949–1959)
400,000 people
The Great Hall of the People (1959)
National Museum of China (1959)
Monument to the People's Heroes (1958)

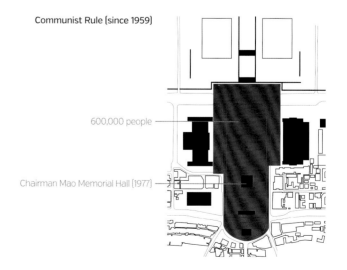

Communist Rule (since 1959)
600,000 people
Chairman Mao Memorial Hall (1977)

located at the eastern edge of the square. Under the Communist rule, public museums in China are seldom about the past. Instead, they are places designed by the Party to tell the story of its assured path of victory and myriad achievements through carefully chosen artifacts, paintings, and sculptures. It is also a classroom to teach youngsters about patriotism and socialist ideals. While the National Museum of China has mounted a variety of shows in recent years (for example, an exhibition of sculptures by Rodin), the centerpiece is a permanent exhibition entitled "The Road of Rejuvenation," which chronicles modern Chinese history from the Opium War to the present day. It highlights Xi Jinping's "China's Dream" – his signature call for national revival and the transformation of China into a strong nation. The museum exhibits do not assess modern Chinese history in its diversity and complexity (such as the devastating civil war between the CCP and its archrival Nationalist Party) or recount domestic calamities (such as the great famine of the late 1950s and the Cultural Revolution of the mid- 1960s). Instead, their purpose, according to the official guidebook, is to show how the CCP "led people from all ethnicities to fight for independence, liberation, prosperity, and well-being."[2] My January 2015 visit to the museum coincided with a major show on "Modern Chinese Masterpieces" from the museum's own collection. Placed in the center hall on the ground floor is Dong Xiwen's celebrated oil painting, *The Founding Ceremony of the Nation* (1953), which depicts Mao's declaration of the founding of the PRC in October 1949 atop Tiananmen Gate – another visual reminder that the CCP brought blissful life to the Chinese people.

Politics

Above all, Tiananmen Square serves as an ideal theatrical stage for the CCP. It is here where major national policies are set and future plans announced. They are elaborately planned and ceremonially executed in the Great Hall of the People, the grandest of all of the monumental buildings in the square—"the crown among the most important of them," as Chinese officials call it—constructed in 1959 to celebrate the nation's 10th anniversary. In this temple of power, full sessions of the National People's Congress meet every March to deliberate on state matters. Even more important, delegates to the National Congress of the Chinese Communist Party assemble in the hall once every five years, since 1977, to chart its ideological course. One should

never forget who is in charge. All the decisions in this building are issued officially under the directive of "the leaders of the Party and the government" (*dang he guojia de lingdaoren*). The message is clear: it is the Chinese Communist Party that is leading the government (Chinese people and their representatives), never the other way around. This proclamation stands against China's constitution, which declares that "all power in the People's Republic of China belongs to the people."[3]

The political influence of Tiananmen Square is not confined to its 44-hectare plaza. It extends to its two immediate adjacent areas that I call "the extended political sphere of Tiananmen Square." The first area is made up of two public parks: Zhongshan Park, northwest of the square, and the park of the Working People's Cultural Palace, northeast of the square. The second area is the parade route of Chang'an Avenue, a distance of four kilometers running in an east–west direction from Dongdan intersection, east of the square, to Xidan intersection, west of the square. This extended sphere serves as a ritualistic route for grand celebrations to take place on national holidays. The two parks and the grand avenue, however, are symptomatic of the CCP's control of the population in a different way: the intrusion of the state into people's private lives.

Zhongshan Park and the Working People's Cultural Palace, two former royal gardens and temples used exclusively by emperors and princes in bygone days, were turned into public parks "for the people" after the Communists came to power.[4] But unlike Western recreational parks where ordinary folk can go for a walk, have a picnic, read, or play games, Chinese Communist parks have a different purpose. In the early decades of the PRC, the Communists frequently expressed contempt for the leisure activities of the bourgeoisie, which were a direct contrast to work, considered the only source of value. Radical Maoists roundly condemned leisure undertakings during the Cultural Revolution. The Communists also feared that urban parks, if unchecked, could be easily turned into subversive gathering places; activities there had to be kept within bounds. At the same time, urban parks are ideal stations to disseminate official messages. Because of their central location, Zhongshan Park and the Working People's Cultural Palace have often been used by the CCP to launch political campaigns (including those opposed to imperialism) and to stage propaganda shows to promote government achievements. One of the continuing official activities at the Working People's Cultural Palace is the promotion of "model workers," labor heroes who contributed to the advancement of collective goals.[5] The appropriation of public parks by the state is an extension of the power of the Party. This has resulted in the encroachment of the state on people's private space.

Chang'an Avenue sees further influence of Tiananmen Square's politics. As Beijing's major boulevard (known as the "Number One Avenue" in China), Chang'an avenue has, since 1949, formed a new east–west axial line that intersects the traditional north–south line in front of Tiananmen Gate. Early on, the Party decided that "Chang'an Avenue must be used to predominantly reflect the capital as the nation's political center."[6] To that end, the section from Dongdan crossing to Xidan crossing was widened extensively in the late 1950s, reaching in some locations 120 meters in width. This is an avenue of formal government buildings. Lining the two sides of the boulevard are the most powerful

Party and state institutions, including the Ministry of Public Security in the east and the Propaganda Department and the Organization Department—both subdivisions of the CCP Central Committee—in the west. Together they form a capsule summation of China's highest power structure.

Even more important, this section serves as the parade route for large processions and national celebratory events. Like the Bolsheviks in Russia, the Chinese Communists are skilled propagandists, who, especially before the Cultural Revolution, used spectacular parades to advance their political goals, primarily on National Day (October 1) and Labor Day (May 1). On National Day, a military march was followed by a "people's parade," with thousands of enthusiastic civilians marching in formations alongside colorful floats from Dongdan to Xidan. Party organizers carefully transformed these carnival-like festivities into a formulaic pageant of military strength, nationalistic fervor, and a paean to the CCP and its leaders. The total number of participants in the parades ranged from

Above: "The Founding Ceremony of the Nation (revised)" (1967) by Dong Xiwen, courtesy of the National Museum of China.

300,000 to half a million. But although these were billed as people's parades, they were in actuality a festivity in praise of the Party. Every facet of the procession was precisely orchestrated by the Party to generate maximum impact for promoting national pride. The crescendo came when paraders filed through Tiananmen Gate, saluting the nation's top leaders and heaping praise on the CCP's most recent achievements – a magical moment when the Party and the people were united as one.

As a parade boulevard, Chang'an Avenue should not be confused with the sort of diverse, boisterous, or even unplanned community street espoused by Jane Jacobs in *The Death and Life of Great American Cities* (1961). A simple walk from Dongdan to Xidan can be a taxing experience. The boulevard is not fit for pedestrians: there are few trees to shield one from the scorching summer sun or the freezing winter wind, nor are there roadside benches for a tired stroller to take a rest. The towering government blocks rise without a community neighborhood, and the avenue's preoccupation with solemnity and rigid standardization makes the place dull and even lifeless. In designing it as a political street, the Communists sacrificed humanity for high politics, undermining community sentimentality and sapping social vitality out of the thoroughfare. Chang'an Avenue is a people's street where public life has been swept away. It is a classic example of how politics usurped city life, turning a citizen space into a propaganda hyperbole.

Conclusion

Tiananmen Square is not static. It is a contemporary government showroom constantly renewing itself. Here is perhaps the best place in the nation to catch a first glimpse of the latest political trends in China. The 56 gigantic red columns placed in the square during the Beijing Olympics in 2008 projected the image of unity and harmony among all ethnic groups in China, mirroring the leaders' deep worry about heightened tensions in minority regions such as Tibet and Xinjiang. The two giant outdoor LED screens situated in the square from 2009 until 2014 were high-tech devices for broadcasting the Party's goal of cultivating "core values of socialism." Flashing across the screens, in lively graphics and text, were phrases such as "socialism is good," "patriotism," "harmony," "democracy," and "filial piety" (an old Confucian value making a comeback). These tired slogans, when aired in this magic political stage, seemed to gain a new lease on life.

Tiananmen Square is a scripted text. Here, the raising of the national flag every morning, the parades, and the regular assembling of delegates in the Great Hall of the People are required readings in a textbook written at the top – predictable and safe. Yet it is the unscripted part–the spontaneous voices of the people–that bring the greatest fear to the leaders.

By definition, a "people's square" should not belong to any political party or be affiliated with any interest group. It belongs to ordinary citizens, which means that it can belong to nobody in particular. Thus, the people have the right to take it back, especially when opportunities arise. This tension between the CCP, which claims to represent the people, and the people themselves can result in violent and tragic consequences. In April 1976, during the traditional Qingming Festival where the living pay tribute to their ancestors by tending family graves, thousands flocked to the square in an outpouring of grief to lay wreaths at the Monument to the People's Heroes in honor of Premier Zhou Enlai, who had died a few months earlier. The gatherings soon turned into an unplanned demonstration against the radical Maoists, later known as the Gang of Four. The ensuing riots and mass arrests were an indication of the distrust and hostility between the government and the governed. In June 1989, people again gathered at the square to commemorate the passing of Hu Yaobang, the deposed but highly respected CCP general secretary. This soon turned into a protest against corruption in the government and a demand for a democratic system. The brutal suppression of the unarmed demonstrators (mostly students) on June 4 by the People's Liberation Army, ordered by senior Party leaders, was another example of the battle between the people and the Party over control of the square. Confrontations will no doubt continue in the future in this "people's square." To suppress any threat to its rule, the CCP must keep the square under tight control. Ironically, Tiananmen Square is one of the world's largest open spaces, yet it is also one of the most restricted.

1 For a brief history of Tiananmen Square, see Chang-tai Hung, *Mao's New World: Political Culture in the Early People's Republic* (Ithaca: Cornell University Press, 2011), 25–50.

2 The National Museum of China, *Exhibition News*, 2015 (January 2015), no. 41.

3 "Chapter 1, General Principles, Article 2," *Constitution of the People's Republic of China* (amendment, March 14, 2004).

4 Zhongshan Park's predecessor was the Imperial Altar of Land and Grain, which had already been turned into a public park called Central Park in 1914, after the collapse of the Qing dynasty. In 1928 it was renamed Zhongshan Park to commemorate Dr. Sun Yat-sen (Sun Zhongshan), the foremost revolutionary leader of the Republic of China. The predecessor of the Working People's Cultural Palace was the Imperial Ancestral Temple, a shrine where Ming and Qing emperors offered sacrifices to their ancestors on special occasions. It assumed its present name in 1950, after the Communist takeover.

5 "Guanyu zai shoudu ge gongyuan nei sheli laodong mofan ji zhandou yingxiong shiji tupian huiyi de jilu" [Record of the meeting on displaying photos of model workers and heroic soldiers in the capital's public parks] (1955), *Beijing Municipal Archives*, 153-1-1238.

6 "Guanyu Chang'anjie gaijian guihua sheji gongzuo qingkuang de baogao" [A report on the reconstruction and planning of Chang'an Avenue] (1964), *Beijing Municipal Archives*, 131-1-139.

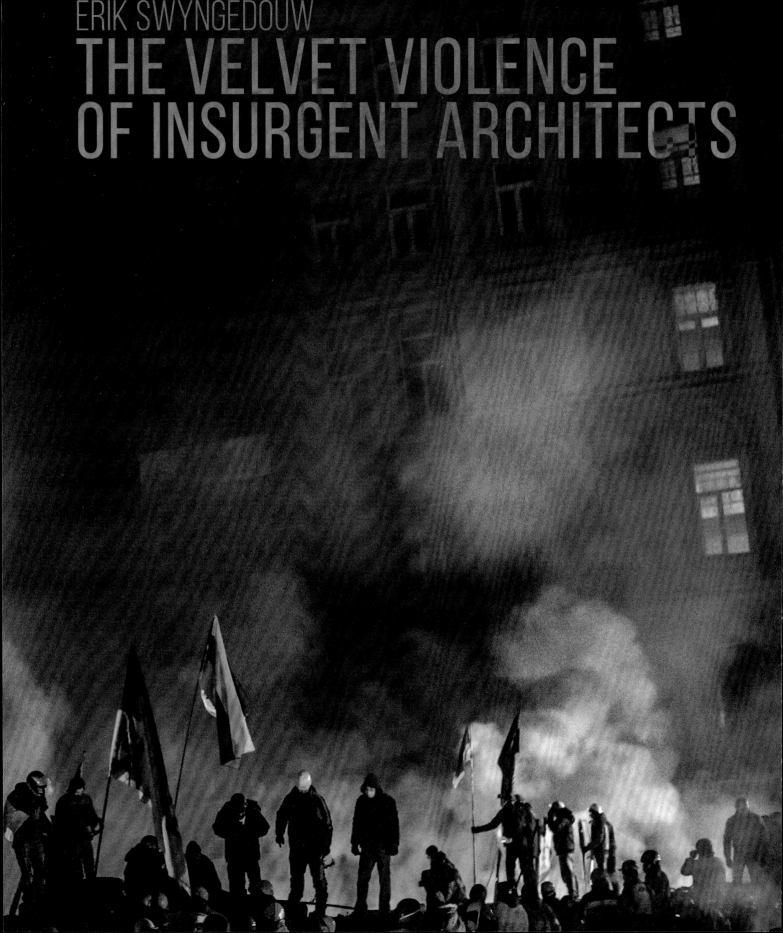

ERIK SWYNGEDOUW

THE VELVET VIOLENCE
OF INSURGENT ARCHITECTS

Erik Swyngedouw is Professor of Geography at Manchester University, UK. His research interests include political-ecology, hydro-social conflict, urban governance and urban movements, democracy and political power, and the politics of globalization. Swyngedouw was previously Professor of Geography at Oxford University and is author of several books including *Social Power and the Urbanization of Water* (2004), *Designing the Post-Political City and the Insurgent Polis* (2011), and *Liquid Power* (2015). He recently co-edited (with Japhy Willson) *The Post-Political and its Discontents* (2014).

+ POLITICAL SCIENCE, URBAN STUDIES, GEOGRAPHY

2011 was an extraordinary urban year. Not since the 1960s have so many people in vastly different cities across the world taken to the streets, occupying squares and experimenting with new ways of organizing the urban commons. There is indeed an uncanny choreographic affinity between the eruptions of discontent that continue to dot the urban landscape and have shaken cities as diverse as Istanbul, Cairo, Tunis, Athens, Madrid, Lyon, Lisbon, Rome, New York, Tel Aviv, Santiago, Chicago, London, Berlin, Frankfurt, Thessaloniki, Stockholm, Barcelona, Montreal, Frankfurt, Oakland, Sao Paulo, or Rio de Janeiro, among many others. A wave of deeply political protest rolls through the world's cities, whereby those who do not count demand a new constituent process for producing space politically. Under the generic names of 'Real Democracy Now,' '*Indignados*,' or 'Occupy!,' the heterogeneous mix of gatherers expose the variegated 'wrongs' and spiraling inequalities of neoliberalization and instituted post-democratic governance.[1]

These insurgent architects—understood as the heterogeneous group of gatherers that express deep discontent with the existing situation and assemble to experiment with and tentatively prefigure new democratizing urban public spaces—signal how the political might re-emerge as an immanent practice within the production of urban space. These rebels act politically within concrete, but deeply contested, social and spatial configurations. In the process, they reconsider and rearticulate their allocated function and location within the common-sense arrangements of everyday life and aspire to forging a new sense of being and belonging.

Emancipatory urban politics cannot be other than a practice, a set of affective and sequential acts that require painstaking organization, careful thought, radical imagination and, above all, the intellectual and political courage to inaugurate an equal,

solidarity-based, and free socio-spatial order that abolishes what exists and produces the new within the interstitial spaces of the old. The historically enduring markers of such an emancipatory political sequence revolve around the notions of equality, freedom, solidarity, and the democratic management of the socio-ecological commons of life.

Messages from Insurgent Architects

Alain Badiou argued recently that we are indeed living in "a time of riots."[2] These spectacular, decidedly urban–albeit ephemeral–outbursts of political desires exploded alongside the proliferation of more enduring, slow, often less visible, socio-spatial and socio-ecological experimentations with new forms of urbanism visible in all manner of new urban commons like occupied houses in Spain, new collectives of solidarity in Athens, or urban laboratories for new forms of production. Do these variegated urban insurgencies not signal a clarion call to return the architectural and urban intellectual gaze to consider again what the polis has always been, namely the site for political encounter and place for enacting the new, the improbable, things often considered impossible by those who do not wish to see any change, the site for production of new radical imaginaries for what urban democratic being-in-common might be all about and what forms it might take?

For Alain Badiou (as well as Jacques Rancière), the democratic political is predicated upon the egalitarian capacity of each and all to act politically. It is a site open for occupation by those who call it into being, claim it, and stage 'equality' in the face of the actually existing inequalities that mark the present condition, irrespective of the 'place' they occupy within the social fabric.

Re-thinking the political is vital, I maintain, for an emancipatory project in a contemporary urban condition that is characterized by a post-politicizing police order that manages the spatial allocation, distribution, and circulation of things and people through a consensually agreed neoliberal arrangement.[3] The political as a space for nurturing dissensus is thereby foreclosed.[4] These techno-managerial state practices and policy procedures colonize and evacuate the political from everyday space.[5] Spatialized policies (planning, architecture, urban policies, etc.) are among the core dispositives of such post-politicizing governing. Post-politicization is a process by which a consensus has been built around the inevitability of state-backed capitalism as an economic system, parliamentary democracy as the political ideal, and humanitarianism and inclusive cosmopolitanism as its moral foundation. Such consensual bio-political governmentality either disavows fundamental conflict or elevates it to the violence of ethnicized antithetical ultra-politics.

The post-political consensus is therefore one that is radically reactionary, that forestalls the articulation of divergent, conflicting, and alternative trajectories of future urban possibilities and assemblages. The Bolivarian alternative and its political support in urban social movements, the articulation

between urban movements and wider forms of politicization as currently practiced by Syriza in Greece, Podemos in Spain (with recent electoral successes in Barcelona and Madrid), or the Right to the City movement in Poland are such tentative experiments that invariably meet with the scorn of both local and global elites. However, consensus does not equal peace or absence of fundamental conflict,[6] but disavows, if not forecloses, the inherent antagonisms inscribed in the self-expansion of value in capitalist circuits of production and exchange. Such post-democratic configuration is often confronted with a variety of 'tactics of resistance.' These are the spheres where an impotent urban activism dwells as some form for 'placebo' politicalness,[7] where disagreements, contestations, and fractures that inevitably erupt out of the incomplete saturation of the social world by the police order are elevated to the dignity of political interruption. For example, the variegated, dispersed, and occasionally effective forms of urban activism and movements that emerge within concrete localized socio-spatial interventions (such as around land-use, pollution problems, road proposals and transport issues, urban development schemes and architectural projects, airport noise, tree felling, industrial works, etc.) elevate localized particular groups and/or organizations to the level of the political, but without universalizing aspirations. These particular forms of hysterical acting out become imbued with political significance. The space of the political is thereby "reduced to the seeming politicization of these groups... Here the political is not truly political because of the restricted nature of the constituency."[8]

Rather than politicizing, such social colonization of the political in fact erodes and outflanks the political dimension of ega-libertarian universalization. The latter cannot be substituted by a proliferation of identitarian, multiple, and ultimately fragmented communities. Moreover, such expressions of protest, that are framed fully within the existing practices and police order, are, in the current post-political arrangement, already fully acknowledged and accounted for.

Emancipatory politicization, in contrast, re-frames what is regarded as political. It inaugurates the repartitioning of the logic of the police, the reordering of what is visible and audible, and registers as voice what was only registered as noise. It occurs in places not allocated to the exercise of power or the instituted negotiation of recognized differences and interests. As Badiou insists, politics emerges as an event in the singular act of choreographing egalitarian appearance of being-in-common that unfolds at a distance from the State. The political is, therefore, about enunciating dissent and rupture. It is literally about voicing speech that claims a place in the order of things, demanding "the part of those who have no-part."[9] It is the arena in which the anarchic noise of the rabble (the part of no-part)– the excluded, disenfranchised, precarious, undocumented, marginalized–is turned into the recognized voice of the People. The political is, therefore, always disruptive. It emerges with the "refusal to observe the 'place' allocated to people and things."[10] It is the terrain where the axiomatic democratic principle of equality is tested in the face of a wrong. Politically, "[e]quality is not something to be researched or verified by critical or other social theory or philosophy but a principle to be upheld."[11] Equality is neither some sort of utopian longing (as is implicit in much of critical urban and architectural theory) nor a sociological concept that can be verified and tested ex-post. It is, in contrast, the very condition upon which the democratic political is contingently and axiomatically founded. The political becomes, for Žižek and Rancière, the space of litigation,[12] the space of those who are uncounted and unnamed, but in their acting stage and demonstrate equality.

Political Designs?

The insurgent architects I mentioned above point to a horizon—a possibility—beyond resistance. While staging equality in public squares is a vital moment, the process of transformation requires the slow but unstoppable production of new forms of spatialization quilted around materializing the claims of equality, freedom, and solidarity. In other words, what is required now and what needs to be thought through is if and how these proto-political insurgent events can turn into a spatialized political procedure. This raises the question of political subjectivation and organizational configurations, and requires perhaps forging a new political Name that captures the imaginary of and desire for an ega-libertarian commons appropriate for the 21st century's forms of planetary urbanization.

The urgent tasks now for those who maintain fidelity to the political events choreographed in the new insurrectional spaces revolve around inventing new practices of collective and sustained political mobilization, organizing the concrete modalities of spatializing and universalizing the Idea (provisionally materialized in these intense and contracted localized insurrectional events), and assembling a wide range of new political subjects who are not afraid to imagine a different commons, demand the impossible, and confront the violence that will inevitably intensify as those who insist on maintaining the present order realize that their days might be numbered.

For Alain Badiou, "a change of world is real when an inexistent of the world starts to exist in the same world with maximum intensity."[13] The order of the sensible is shaken, and the kernel for a new common sense—a new mode of being in common— becomes present in the world and makes its presence common-sens(e)ible. It is the appearance of another world in the world. This is precisely what the sprawling urban insurgents and rebellions have achieved, by igniting a new sensibility about the polis as a democratic and potentially democratizing space. The tidal wave of urban protests shattered the post-political idyll of an unfractured society that recognizes the identitarian claims and demands of its members and organizes a consensually negotiated democratic compromise without any remainders. These protests stand for the dictatorship of the democratic—direct and egalitarian—against the despotism of the 'democracy' of the elites: representative and inegalitarian.[14]

The urban insurgents turned the particular grievances that ignited the events (a threatened park, an urban spectacle like the soccer world championship, radical austerity measures, etc.) into a wholesale attack on the instituted order, on the unbridled commodification of urban life in the interests of the few, on the unequal choreographies of actually existing representational democracy. The particular demands transformed seamlessly into a universalizing staging for something different: however diffuse, inchoate, and unarticulated this may presently be. The assembled groups ended up without particular demands and thereby demanded everything, nothing less then the transformation of the instituted order. They staged new ways of practicing equality and democracy, experimented with innovative and creative ways of being together in the city, and prefigured (both in practice and in theory) new ways of distributing goods, accessing services, producing healthy environments, managing space, constructing artifacts, organizing debate, managing conflict, being-in-common, practicing ecologically saner life-styles, and negotiating urban space in an emancipatory manner.

In the aftermath of these insurgencies, a range of new socio-spatial practices are subject to experimentation, from housing occupations and movements against dispossession in Spain to new ega-libertarian lifestyles and forms of social and ecological organization, alongside more traditional forms of political organizing (visible in the success of Syriza in Greece or of Podemos in Spain). An extraordinary experimentation with dispossessing the dispossessor, with reclaiming the commons and organizing access, transformation, and distribution in more ega-libertarian ways marks the return to 'ordinary' life in the aftermath of the insurgencies. These incipient ideas materialize in a variety of places and practices, in the midst of painstaking efforts to build alliances, bridge sites, repeat the insurgencies, establish connectivities and, in the process, produce organization and generalize desire. Such procedures demand painstaking organization, sustained political action, militant organization, imaginative urban designs, and a committed fidelity to universalizing the egalitarian trajectory for the management of the commons.

These are truly velvet violent encounters and always constitute a political act, one that can be legitimised only in political terms, and not–as is customarily done–through an externalised legitimation that resides in a fantasy of a cohesive city, an 'emancipatory' architecture, or 'sustainable' urban design practice. Any political or architectural act is one that reorders socio-ecological coordinates and patterns, reconfigures uneven socio-ecological relations – often with unforeseen or unforeseeable consequences. It expresses a choice, takes sides, invariably signals a totalitarian moment and the temporary suspension of the democratic, understood as the agonistic encounter of heterogeneous views under the aegis of a presumed equality of all. The gap between the democratic moment and the autocratic moment (as the (temporary) suspension of the democratic) needs to be radically endorsed.

While the democratic political, founded on a presumption of equality, insists on difference, disagreement, radical openness, and exploring multiple possible futures, concrete spatial-ecological intervention is necessarily about relative closure (for some), definitive choice, singular intervention and, thus, certain exclusion and occasionally even outright silencing. Frantz Fanon recognized a long time ago that the objective and real violence of oppression invariably meets the subjective violence of the oppressed in their quest for a more ega-libertarian polis.[15]

1 Japhy Wilson & Erik Swyngedouw (eds.), *The Post-Political and its Discontents* (Edinburgh: Edinburgh University Press, 2014).

2 Alain Badiou, *The Rebirth of History: Times of Riots and Uprisings* (London: Verso, 2012).

3 Erik Swyngedouw, "The Post-Political City," in BAVO (ed.) *Urban Politics Now. Re-imagining Democracy in the Neo-Liberal City* (Rotterdam: NAI-Publishers, 2008), 58–76.

4 Wilson & Swyngedouw, *The Post-Political and its Discontents*.

5 Jacques Rancière, "Dissenting Words. A Conversation with Jacques Rancière (with Davide Panagia)," *Diacritics* 30 (2002): 113–26.

6 Jacques Rancière, *La Haine de la Démocratie* (Paris: La Fabrique, 2005), 8.

7 Olivier Marchart, *Post-Foundational Political Thought – Political Difference in Nancy, Lefort, Badiou and Laclau* (Edinburgh: Edinburgh University Press, 2007), 47.

8 Ibid.

9 Jacques Rancière, "Ten Theses on Politics," *Theory & Event* 5 (2001): 6.

10 Mark Robson, "Introduction: Hearing Voices," *Paragraph* 28 (2005): 5.

11 Peter Hallward, *Badiou – A Subject to Truth* (Minneapolis: University of Minnesota Press, 2003), 228.

12 Savoj Žižek, *The Ticklish Subject – The Absent Centre of Political Ontology* (London: Verso, 1999).

13 Badiou, *The Rebirth of History*, 56.

14 Ibid.

15 Frantz Fanon, *The Wretched of the Earth* (New York: Grove Press, 1963).

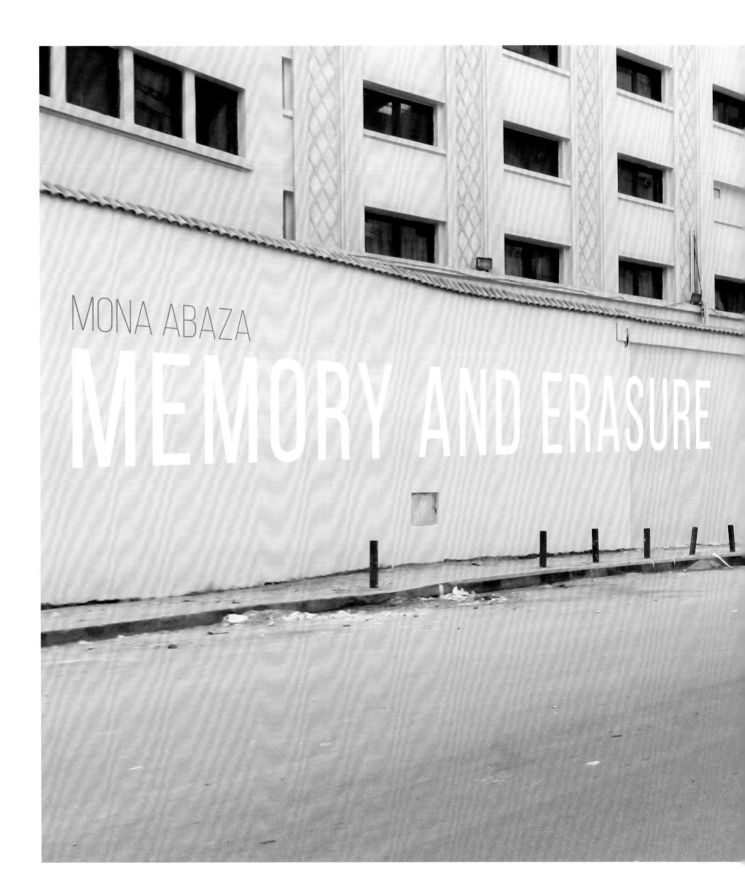

MONA ABAZA

MEMORY AND ERASURE

Mona Abaza is Professor of Sociology at the American University in Cairo. She was previously a visiting professor of Islamology in the Department of Theology at Lund University (2009–2011) and has been a visiting scholar at universities in Singapore, Malaysia, Germany, France, Italy, and The Netherlands. Abaza is author of six books including *The Changing Consumer Culture of Modern Egypt, Cairo's Urban Reshaping* (2006) and *Twentieth Century Egyptian Art: The Private Collection of Sherwet Shafei* (2011).

✚ SOCIOLOGY, PUBLIC ART, POLITICS

How awkward it is to write after the event. In particular, if one is caught in the dilemma of an incomplete revolution; perhaps too, while still struggling with a counter-revolutionary moment. The mesmerizing murals and graffiti shown world-over in the background of the footage of the January 2011 Egyptian revolution and the continuing protests that formed part of the so-called "Arab Spring" have now been erased. Practically no new graffiti has appeared in Cairo this past year.[1] The walls of the city have been whitewashed by the authorities or have been sprayed over by a black paint. Evidently, the carnivalesque moment of January 2011, which caught the attention of numerous observers and which lasted for almost four years, has withered away.

The Arab Spring, first sparked in Tunisia by a destitute and humiliated street vendor who committed the act of self-immolation, resulted in an unprecedented historic replication of rebellions during 2011 against the rule of dictatorship and injustice in various regions of the Middle East. This revolutionary 'virus' that led to the ousting of dictatorial regimes in Tunisia, Egypt, Libya, and Yemen, will be remembered for two spectacular transformations. First, these insurrections opened a novel path in imagining and reinventing the worth of occupying public spaces as performative, carnivalesque, and satirical sites of contestation, generating then much discussion about the role of social media in blending the virtual world with very urban militarized wars and violent confrontations. And second, the Egyptian revolution (perhaps more than any other) spawned a veritable "tsunami" of visual media, to paraphrase WJT Mitchell,[2] thus raising challenges regarding the urgency of information storage and classification in counter-revolutionary moments working precisely on the erasure of memory. In Cairo, the blooming of street art has been part and parcel of this novel visual public articulation.

"Sharei' uyuun al-hurriyyah" (the street of the eyes of freedom), and "the street of the Martyrs," were nicknames given to Mohammed Mahmoud Street, one of the main streets leading to Cairo's Tahrir Square, which featured in many images of the 2011–2012 uprising. This street is memorable for having witnessed some of the most dramatic and violent moments of the uprising, but it is also remembered as the site of some of the most mesmerizing revolutionary graffiti in the city.

During the entire year of 2011, the walls of Mohammed Mahmoud Street underwent fantastic mutations on a weekly basis, epitomized in a constant war that entailed the painting of walls, erasure by the authorities, and repainting over and over again by numerous graffiti artists.[3] Apart from ironic content, the theme of commemorating the martyrs is what is most moving about these murals. Much attention has been drawn to the appearance, disappearance, and reappearance of the numerous faces and portraits of the martyrs of the revolution. Underneath each martyr, the date and location of the incident causing their death is written. As Egyptian authorities kept erasing the art by whitening the walls, artists responded with more-elaborate and sometimes improved versions of the previous paintings, itself an art of resistance. As if one could draw entire galleries filled with ever increasing portraits of the dead.

Now, some four years since, we see the emerging commodification of revolutionary street art, with graffiti artists being represented by reputable galleries, and adopted by established curators and art centers. Some such artists have been commissioned to reproduce the "street," repainting entire murals and walls of graffiti in gallery and art spaces in Cairo's downtown. This commodification of revolutionary art has sparked tensions among artists, while resulting in a boom in elitist galleries discovering how lucrative revolutionary art can be.

But rather than lamenting the rampant commodification of revolutionary art, let us focus on one of the main problems encountered today by those who still have faith in change for a better future. Many in Egypt today believe that recording and archiving the "collective memory" of the past four years of events unfolding since the January 2011 revolution constitutes *the* battle against the pervasive official propaganda machinery. As Sherief Gaber argued recently, for those who still maintain faith in the revolutionary path, the decisive struggle today is evolving around "political memory" in times of powerful smear campaigns against activists and human rights advocates.[4] This short piece is a modest endeavor in the battle between memory and erasure, to provide a record of a cultural moment that has already disappeared.

1 With the exception of a much controversial recent initiative launched by Swedish journalist Mia Gröndahl, who organized for female graffiti artists to paint over the graffiti on the walls of the former library of the American University in Youssef al-Guindi Street. This project resulted into an open war with the graffiti artists who had previously painted on that same wall a satirical portrait of Gröndahl figuring with Euros and dollars on her open chest. See, Ilka Eickhof "Graffiti, Capital and Deciding what's Inappropriate," *Mada Masr* (April 7, 2015).

2 W.J.T. Mitchell, "Image, Space, Revolution: The Arts of Occupation," *Critical Inquiry* 39, no. 1 (2012): 8–32, 14.

3 Mona Abaza, "An Emerging Memorial Space? In Praise of Mohammed Mahmud Street," *Jadaliyya* (March 10, 2012).

4 Sherief Gaber, Middle East Center AUC, "Mosireen and the Battle for Political Memory" (2014), http://www.jadaliyya.com/pages/index/16616/mosireen-and-the-battle-for-political-memory (accessed January 4, 2015).

The Potsdamer Platz

1920 Potsdamer Platz—a cultural, commercial, and transport hub at the geographical center of Berlin—is renowned as Europe's most exciting urban place.

1933 Adolf Hitler becomes chancellor of Germany and moves into the Chancellery, one block north of Potsdamer Platz.

1937 Hitler and his architect Albert Speer release plans for redeveloping Berlin as "Germania," the new world capital. The north–south axis of this scheme runs just west of Potsdamer Platz.

1939 The new Reich Chancellory, the office of the chanellor of Germany, is completed. The massive building designed by Speer is four hundred meters long and twenty meters high.

1943 The buildings surrounding Potsdamer Platz are devastated by air raids.

1945 Hitler takes up residence in the Führerbunker behind the Chancellery where, at midnight on April 28, he marries Eva Braun. Two days later, upon hearing of the imminent arrival of Soviet forces, Hitler and Braun commit suicide (marked as ✚ on the 1937 plan).

1945 Soviet forces arrive in Potsdamer Platz on May 1, followed two months later by the American, French, and British forces. Berlin is divided into four sectors representing these nations, with Potsdamer Platz becoming the dividing line between the eastern (Russian) and western (French, American, and British) sectors.

1948 The western sectors (known as West Berlin) are encircled by the creation of East Germany, supported by the Soviet Union. Rendered inaccessible by land, West Berliners are kept alive with supplies airlifted from the West.

1949 The USSR lifts the blockade of West Berlin.

1953 East Berliners protest on Potsdamer Platz against the "Sovietization" of East Germany. Riots are violently suppressed by Soviet troops and tanks.

1955 Russia grants sovereignty to the German Democratic Republic (East Germany).

1956 Remnant buildings around Leipziger Platz and Potsdamer Platz are demolished.

1957 Several urban design competitions are conducted for the reconstruction of the center of Berlin. Entries by Le Corbusier and the Smithsons favor a modernist tabular rasa approach.

1961 East Germany seals off West Berlin by constructing a barrier that becomes known as the Berlin Wall. Over time it becomes two walls defining a "no-man's-land" in between.

1963 President Kennedy visits the Berlin Wall at Potsdamer Platz to challenge Soviet oppression and declares "Ich bin ein Berliner." This translates literally as "I am a Berlin donut," but everyone knew what he meant.

1963 A series of cultural buildings begin construction in West Berlin, just west of Potsdamer Platz, including Hans Scharoun's Berlin Philharmonic Hall and Mies van der Rohe's National Gallery.

1979 The West Berlin International Building Exhibition (IBA) begins with the obvious intent of producing landmark designs to signal to the east that the west continued to prosper.

1980 West Berliners begin converting the west-facing wall into the world's longest mural.

1987 Ronald Reagan makes his "tear down this wall" speech anticipating Gorbachev's relaxation of socialism in the USSR.

1989 On November 9 the East German government formally allows its citizens free passage into the West. Hundreds of thousands surge to West Berlin, smashing down the Wall.

1990 Berlin is re-established as the capital of a united Germany. Potsdamer Platz is a field of rubble and the name comes to describe an amorphous, large area of empty land in the center of a united Berlin where impromptu events take place.

1991 A shortlisted design competition for the future of Potsdamer Platz is won by Munich architects Himmler and Sattler. Daimler Benz and Richard Rogers produce and exhibit an uninvited alternative scheme.

1992 Not without controversy, a second design competition is held and won by Renzo Piano and Christoph Kohlbecker. The masterplan by Himmler and Sattler is subsequently parceled up to Daimler Benz, Sony, MetroAG and their various architects: Renzo Piano, Helmut Jahn, Hans Kollhoff, Arata Isozaki, Oswald Mathias Ungers, Rafael Moneo, and Richard Rogers.

1996 A landscape competition for the public spaces of Potsdamer Platz is won by Gross Max.

2004 The memorial to the murdered Jews of Europe, a field of 2,117 concrete stelae by architect Peter Eisenman and sculptor Richard Serra is unveiled just north of Potsdamer Platz.

2015 Sony and Daimler Benz have sold their Potsdamer Platz properties, the public spaces (apart from Peter Walker's semi-public Sony Centre work) are in a state of incompletion and disrepair. The place where Hitler committed suicide is now part of the landscape of an unremarkable residential development. Berliners generally stay well away from the area.

Sources: Alan Balfour, Berlin: *The Politics of Order* (New York: Rizzoli, 1990); Harold Bodenschatz, *Berlin Urban Design* (Berlin: DOM, 2010); Vittorio Magnago Lampugnani & Romana Schneider, *Einstuck Grosstadt als Experiment Planungen am Potsdamer Platz in Berlin* (Stuttgart: Verlag Gerd Halse, 1994).

1920

1937

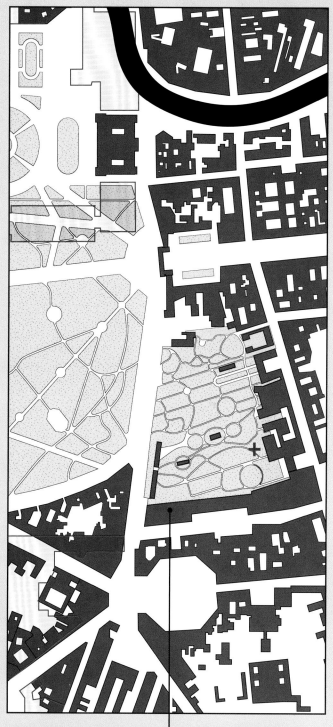

POTSDAMER PLATZ ———

 SPEER'S GERMANIA ——— REICH CHANCELLERY

✚ HITLER'S BUNKER

1948

1961

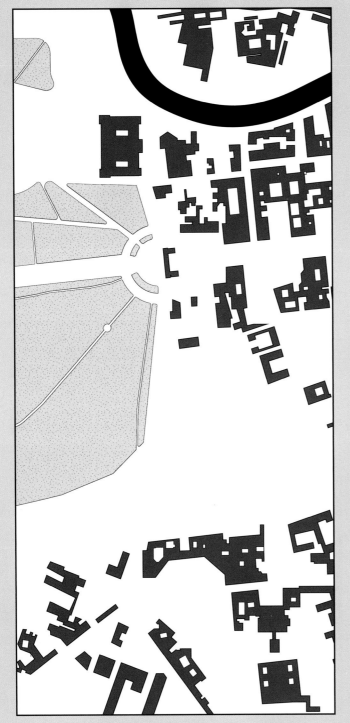

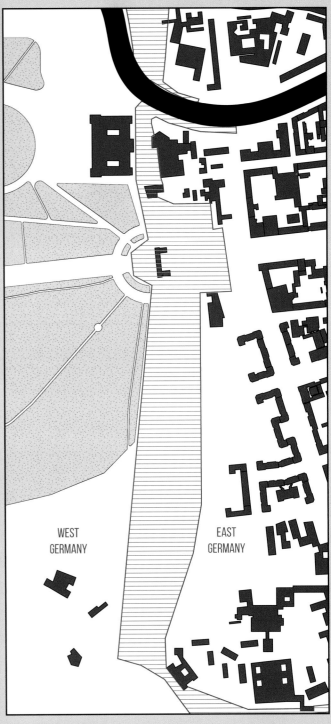

WEST
GERMANY

EAST
GERMANY

NO MAN'S LAND

1990

2015

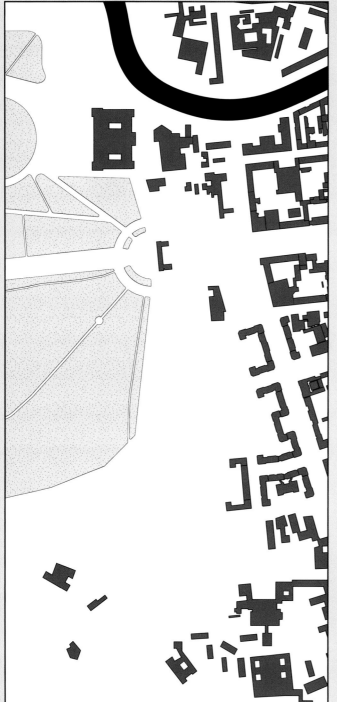

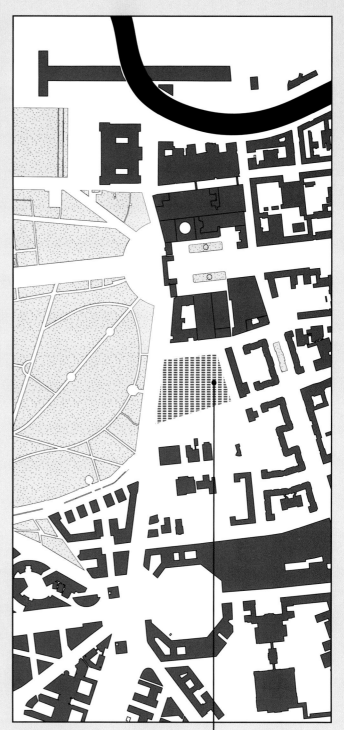

MEMORIAL TO THE MURDERED JEWS OF EUROPE

JESSE KRIMES
APOKALUPTEIN:16389067:II

Jesse Krimes was indicted in 2009 on non-violent drug charges and sentenced to a 70-month prison term, during which time he was known as "prisoner 16389067." While incarcerated, Krimes produced several bodies of work, established art programs, and worked collaboratively with his fellow inmates. Krimes' work investigates the human condition seeking to disentangle complex value systems and hierarchies, and challenge dominant representations. Krimes holds a BA in Studio Art from Millersville University.

✛ VISUAL ARTS

Apokaluptein:16389067:II, installed in Philadelphia's decommissioned Eastern State Penitentiary, is a recreation by artist Jesse Krimes of an original work made while he served six years in a US federal prison for non-violent drug crimes. The work—which consists of newspaper images transferred onto prison bed sheets, blended and linked using color pencil and graphite—highlights Eastern State Penitentiary's architectural design and its ideological foundation in seeking penance through silent and solitary religious contemplation. The cell's single skylight, representing the "Eye of God," directly references Jeremy Bentham's Panopticon, suggesting the omnipresence of God and Government. This power dynamic, in addition to the strict solitary confinement practiced at Eastern State Penitentiary, exerted immense pressure on inmates' mental health and self-identity. The system of solitary confinement was practiced at Eastern State Penitentiary from its inception in 1829 to 1905 when "more humane" methods of confinement permitting limited prisoner congregation were introduced.

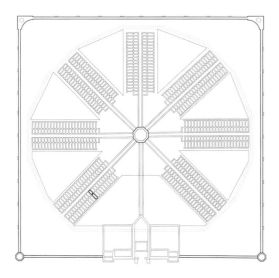

Opposite: *Apokaluptein:16389067:II*, 2015, Jesse Krimes (15'x8'x18' artwork installation at Eastern State Penitentiary, Philadelphia, USA).

Plan of Eastern State Penitentiary (1830), showing location of installation in red.

RODRIGO JOSÉ FIRMINO

CONNECTED AND CONTROLLED

SURVEILLANCE, SECURITY, AND CITIES

I will begin by listing a few words that represent most of what this article has to say about cities and technology in the 21st century and beyond. These words are in our thoughts about (and shaping the design of) the city of the present and those still to come. Most of these words have already become familiar to us: code, automation, data, surveillance, monitoring, control, connection, smart, and things. Yes, things! Objects, devices, tools, artifacts, utensils, instruments, buildings, infrastructure—whatever we call them—are talking to each other, connecting to one another and taking actions for us, as well as influencing other actions that we perform. They are an influential part of the social fabric that defines contemporary life in an urbanized world.[1]

Obviously, these are all inanimate things that depend on pre-programmed behaviors to do whatever they do. But the important point is that we are incorporating communication capabilities into these inanimate objects (making them 'smarter'), and because we are living in an increasingly codified world with unbearable amounts of data about everything now available, we are also able to automate tasks performed by objects, which are increasingly connected in a network of endless other things. This network in turn performs ever-more complicated, interlinked, automated tasks that allow us to monitor, control, and perform surveillance on ourselves and on activities that influence our daily routines.

The idea of a city of the Internet of things supported by autonomous technologies that can communicate with each other with minimum human mediation is already part of the reality of contemporary urban space. The Internet of things (IoT)—a seamless network of operations and actions triggered by interconnected devices—may in future provide an autonomous cascading development of technological systems that can control urban structures and human actions in the city.

We are witnessing the early days of the programmable city.[2] Our lives, as urban beings, are about to become augmented, but also constrained, by the power of collecting and manipulating unimaginable amounts of information. In the early 1990s, Manuel Castells was busy trying to convince his readers and students that the post-industrial urban milieu was configuring itself in what he called the "informational city."[3] This idea was based on the technological and socioeconomic restructuring of production and consumption chains that was affecting the shape of cities and regions around the world as well as the relations in and between them. I am almost certain that even in his wildest dreams (and studies), Castells would not have imagined what we are starting to experience in terms of data management and its relations with macro and micro spatial processes.

'Automation' and 'smart' are today's buzzwords. Finally, it seems that the dreams of a machine-supported modern way of life and the modernist city are slowly and smoothly coming to life. The famous automated modern house depicted in Jacques Tati's 1958

Rodrigo José Firmino is a Professor in Urban Management at the Pontifical Catholic University in Curitiba, Brazil, and Research Fellow with the Brazil Ministry of Science and Technology. He holds a PhD in Urban Planning from Newcastle University, UK, and an MPhil in Architecture and Urbanism from the University of São Paulo (2000). Since 2004 his research has focused on the co-development of urban and technological strategies for cities in developing countries.

 TECHNOLOGY, URBAN STUDIES

film *Mon Oncle* (*My Uncle*) is being given tangible form, albeit with less irony this time. Urban phantasmagoric depictions of coded life and spaces[4] presented in this and other films like *The Matrix* and *Minority Report* are no longer exaggerated fantasies of a distant future. The immanent ever-present future of cities is getting closer and closer and will charge its price. In a recent article for a series on the IoT in the British newspaper *The Guardian*, Nicole Kobie states that there may be a price to pay for the convenience of a world surrounded by (and dependent on) interconnected smart things:

> It's handy to be able to unlock your door from a distance, but not so convenient if a burglar can do the same [...] And then there's privacy. We already face online surveillance—what happens when even our home appliances add to the pool of personal data collected about us?[5]

It is indisputable that humanity has reached an inescapable level of dependence on technological systems and that these systems are indispensable to the maintenance of current standards of comfort as well as local and global transactions of all kinds. Regarding the intrinsic amalgamated nature of technological development and society, we are the technologies we produce as much as these technologies are us. We, as a society, need to figure out what it is we are building as cities and to decide whether this is what we want or not. Unfortunately, the formula is a bit more complicated and the question of whether we like it this way or not depends on a whole chain of events influenced by interests, negotiations, and power disputes. However, the first issue—figuring out what we are doing—is still available to us as a way of understanding and influencing our futures in the urban world.

I believe it is possible to see this relation between smart technologies and society from a spatial point of view and that this spatial interpretation is, theoretically, directly related to the very concept of territory. In geography, it is plausible to distinguish between territories and places[6] based on the way people relate to their own spaces. Territory and place are not ontological properties of a locale, but individual and collective constructions. This appropriation of space can be influenced by many kinds of relationships between bodies, minds, and the environment: sensorial (involving all five senses), psychological, personal, collective, social, political, and cultural. All these relationships can alter the way we see and feel the space around us. The result of these connections can define what type of territorial association we build among us – whether it is the place we 'belong to' or a territory controlled by 'others' whose constitutional rules we have to accept while we are there.

Locales are constantly reconstituted through appropriation and use in new territorializing processes. The availability of communication and information networks transforms the use of public squares and attracts people to them, in the manner of new urban facilities, such as parks for children or exercise areas for adults. In this sense, the possibilities afforded by 'smarter' cities through processes of 'informational territorialization'[7] are also allowing people (and the state) to shape their own

individual and collective territories in new ways, making the process of constituting formal and informal territories–territorialization–more complex than it has ever been in the past. Differences between public and private spaces, as well as the way we build these spaces, are becoming more blurred, and the concepts of public and private spaces are beginning to overlap more frequently.

There are at least two ways in which this shaping of individual and collective territories can happen, both of which serve different purposes. The first of these is the building of smarter cities as centrally defined, dictated and implemented initiatives, where governments, for example, use all the new technologies in programs to monitor spaces and behaviors in strategic sites throughout a city, inflicting a territorial power upon public places. Built in partnership between IBM and Rio de Janeiro's local government and housed in a building that concentrates officials from over 30 city departments and law-enforcement forces in a single NASA-like control room, the Center of Operations in Rio (COR)[8] is a well-known case where this kind of territorialization is exercised.

Secondly, there are informal, decentralized, and sometimes even underground grassroots movements using the same types of technologies to build their own government-free solutions for real urban problems. This is a rapidly growing phenomenon where ordinary people are empowered by the same kinds of technologies that can be used to destroy their liberties. It has received many different names, from 'crowdsourcing urbanism', to 'pop-up city' or 'DIY city', and examples of the phenomenon are to be found everywhere.

Some of these movements are directly related to the ways in which people build their own places and territories. Brazilian cities have a common transport problem that an ordinary citizen in Europe or North America would find absurd in a modern 21st-century city: most bus stops do not even list which buses stop there. So, a group of 20-something friends (called 'shoot the shit') already involved with other actions to improve services around their hometown, Porto Alegre, used social media and smartphone apps to distribute lists and even stickers that people could print and paste on bus stops. This very simple initiative has since spread to 35 other cities across Brazil, making one wonder why an affordable IoT system has not been implemented on buses and bus stops to provide such simple yet vital information.

Finally, regarding the purpose of building connected spaces in these centralized or decentralized ways, it is obvious that this can be either to make our lives easier, more comfortable and more independent of the various levels of government or to strip us of our privacy, liberty, rights, and the sense of belonging in public spaces. The latter is what makes us worry about any increase in connectivity and controllability in today's spatial relations. Indeed, it is always for us (practitioners, scholars, and citizens) to decide what kind of balance we want between connection and control. In a post called "The city is here for you to use: 100 easy pieces" in his blog Speedbird, urban designer Adam

Greenfield writes that, among many other features of the promises of smarter everything, "[t]he smart city is predicated on a neoliberal political economy, and in particular presents a set of potentials disturbingly consonant with the exercise of authoritarianism."[9]

In today's maximum-surveillance society,[10] every breath we take is coded and has the potential to be monitored, or watched in real time. As most aspects of transactions and interactions nowadays are coded and transmitted as bits and bytes, almost every move we make creates more or less ephemeral records and leaves traces of our activities. In addition, as smart surveillance technologies make more and more use of locative media (geolocation-aware software and hardware supported by GPS or antenna triangulation techniques), so space comes to matter more than ever. Spatial activities are turned into a powerful commodity in the informational smart city.

Surveillance, dataveillance,[11] and the rise of the automated smart, big-data city (or whatever we may call the city that is currently being built) are the ultimate materialization of Gilles Deleuze's[12] society of control with ubiquity, interoperability, invisibility, miniaturization, and pervasiveness working together through sophisticated technologies and enormous quantities of data, all available for governments and corporations to exercise social sorting and targeted marketing.

Smartness and security is always bought through the use of increasingly ubiquitous and pervasive surveillance technologies, the main currencies being privacy and civil rights. Frightened societies that are highly securitized against domestic and external threats result in spaces where any movement is considered suspicious and therefore must be controlled. In such cases, the interconnection between objects, databases, institutions, and individuals produces distributed surveillance in a splintered control regime covering all activities and events around the city.

On the neighborhood scale, the process of place-making goes

beyond the specific features of affection and simple wellbeing created by some artifice of urban design and architecture. Safety mechanisms, increasingly supported by smart IoT-enabled technologies, can help diminish certain local disturbances in order to reaffirm feelings of belonging and thus create a basis for the emergence of a proper sense of place, resulting in extremely securitized environments. In contemporary cities, there seems to be a trend determined by territorial control and power relations to increase local security.[13]

This trend is related to different ways of using digital smart surveillance as a form of informational territorialization. Interest in the protection of public spaces, the sense of place, privacy, personal information, civil rights, and the exercise of 'old-fashioned free citizenship' has lost priority to fear in the contemporary city. Or, as argued by Darren Palmer and Ian Warren,

> the protection of personal information is secondary to the demands of criminal law enforcement, evidence gathering, the prevention of crime and the goal of community protection.[14]

In this smart, digital, securitized, urban world, traditional control strategies such as high walls, barbed wire, electric fences, and guard dogs are being routinely implemented. Territorialization through actions to provide an increasing sense of safety has long been underway but is now subject to an important informational touch: a computerized security system that is able to connect many different types of data-collecting and monitoring devices to one another and to human enterprise in order to control access to the locality (a building, a neighborhood, or an entire city) and the addition of a predefined set of expected behaviors in private and public spaces. These processes of territorialization through surveillance and security mechanisms are directly related to place-making and place-unmaking. That is, while territorialization can produce situations in which a sense of comfort and security is achieved by the mere presence of the devices, their existence and visibility can be a source of disruption and instability for people who

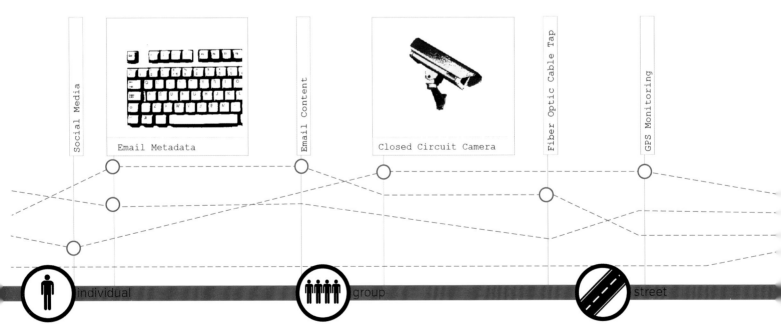

have other relations of place (such as frequent passersby or occasional visitors) within these same locations.

In this context, we can extend this analysis to other forms of surveillance that use the power of big data, automation, and smart interlinked connections (empowered by the IoT) to expand significantly the action of traditional surveillance equipment (such as cameras) to mobile interconnected systems, which are able to locate and identify undesirable situations using sensors, wireless networks and mobile devices. The issues involved in electronic surveillance are related directly to the tension between an informational constitution of controlled territories and the informal and cultural creation of meaningful locales and places, both materially and immaterially.

Taking Brazil again as an example, cities of every size in terms of population and land occupation are being torn apart spatially and socially by the tyranny of urban fear and the resulting rapid spread of highly securitized enclaves (for the rich and poor). This divided space reflects the cellular reproduction upon which urban growth and spatial reproduction is based as peripheral areas are urbanized by the forces of the real estate market. Thus, with the exception of spaces in central areas, urban public space in Brazilian cities is being designed as a leftover place in the process of 'condominiumization' of neighborhoods. Surveillance technologies and practices are playing a silent but persistent role in this process as neighborhoods are dominated by private security companies and the desire of residents for ever-increasing security.

I recently argued in a study about the private video monitoring of public spaces[15] that there is a strong tendency for public space as a place of freedom, and as the people's territory, to disappear. This argument is based on the fact that space in general, and public space in particular, is increasingly vulnerable to control practices by the state and the private sector. The latter is in part supported by new invisible, miniaturized technologies

1 In an Actor-Network Theory approach, we would say that things, like humans, are actants in the networks that form our lives and that this has always been so in the history of human societies. See Bruno Latour, *Reassembling the Social: An Introduction to Actor-Network Theory*. (Oxford: Oxford University Press, 2005).

2 The programmable city: http://www.maynoothuniversity.ie/progcity.

3 Manuel Castells, *The Informational City. Information Technology, Economic Restructuring, and the Urban-Regional Process* (Oxford: Basil Blackwell, 1989).

4 Fábio Duarte, Rodrigo Firmino & Andrei Crestani, "Urban Phantasmagorias: Cinema and the Immanent Future of Cities," *Space and Culture* 18 no. 2 (2014): 132–42.

5 Nicole Kobie, "The Internet of Things: Convenience at a Price," The Guardian: Technology, Connected World (March 30, 2015), http://www.theguardian.com/technology/2015/mar/30/internet-of-things-convenience-price-privacy-security.

6 See for example: Andrea Brighenti, "On Territorology: Towards a General Science of Territory," *Theory, Culture & Society* 27 (2010): 52-72; John Agnew and Stuart Corbridge, *Mastering Space: Hegemony,Territory, and International Political Economy* (London: Routledge, 1995).

7 André Lemos, "Post–Mass Media Functions, Locative Media, and Informational Territories: New Ways of Thinking About Territory, Place, and Mobility in Contemporary Society," *Space and Culture* 13 no. 4 (2010): 403–20.

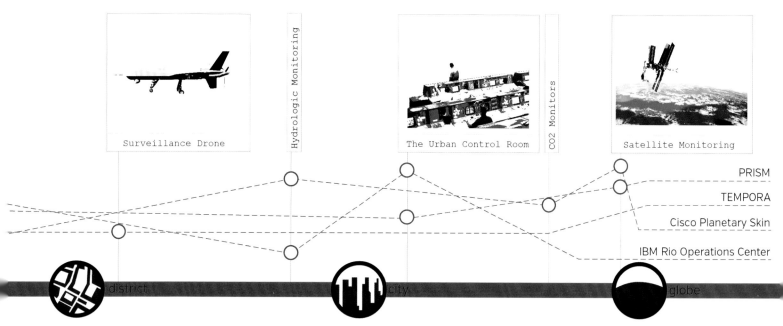

(such as interconnected video surveillance, motion detectors, electronic fences, remote monitoring systems, etc.), and our lack of understanding of what the practices associated with these technologies have implications for the coexistence of differences in the city. In the same study, I pointed out how this invisible expansion of private borders over public locales can interfere in the ways outsiders (to this territory) experience these places under surveillance. There were reports, for instance, where passersby and public services contractors were confronted by private security officers because they were caught on CCTV standing for too long in places where they were 'not supposed to be' (these places being public streets or squares).

In this situation, public space effectively becomes private through the unauthorized surveillance of unknown private actors, often with the tacit acceptance of the state (via the assumption that more surveillance will make public places safer), a condition in which legitimacy for monitoring the public space[16] becomes a central issue. As mentioned above, this is reflected in the fast-growing phenomenon of private surveillance camera systems and networks of residents and private security companies joining efforts to monitor public streets and squares in many Brazilian cities. This has been interpreted[17] as an invisible extension of the boundaries of private territories and control practices over what was supposed to be open public space.

In 2010, the London Metropolitan Police Service launched a counter-terrorism publicity campaign saying: "Don't rely on others. If you suspect it report it." However, I think it is symptomatic that one of the posters used in the campaign showed happy families and CCTV in public places but also tells viewers not to rely on others. We are witnessing the possibility of an increasingly interconnected urban society leading to an obsessive regime of increased security, control, and monitoring. It seems clear that the advent of big data, automation, the IoT, and the phenomena linked to the words I listed in the first paragraph of this paper is related to the way we use spaces and places in cities and mold our contemporary urban experience into an extremely controlled, biased way of life, which ultimately has the potential to compromise what has been the basis for citizenship and has defined public space ever since humans started to live in cities. That is, our capacity to trust and rely on others. Further research into the interplay between surveillance and urban studies is required to question how, by developing increasingly smart cities, we may also be dumbing down future citizens.

I tend to agree with Rem Koolhaas when he suggests in his article "My Thoughts on the Smart City"[18] that to plan, design, and experience a more vivid, human, and respectful city, we will have to change the urban lexicon from that of the smart entrepreneur back to that of the architect, designer, and urbanist.

8 COR's official website: http://www.rio.rj.gov.br/web/corio.

9 Adam Greenfield, "The City Is Here For You To Use: 100 easy pieces," *Speedbird* (December 3rd, 2012), https://speedbird.wordpress.com/2012/12/03/the-city-is-here-for-you-to-use-100-easy-pieces.

10 Clive Norris & Gary Armstrong, *The Maximum Surveillance Society: The Rise of CCTV* (Oxford: Berg, 1999).

11 Roger Clarke, "Information Technology and Dataveillance," *Communications of the ACM* 31 no. 5 (1988): 498–512.

12 Gilles Deleuze, *Postscripts on the Societies of Control* (Cambridge: MIT Press, 1992).

13 Rodrigo Firmino, et al., "Fear, Security, and the Spread of CCTV in Brazilian Cities: Legislation, Debate, and the Market," *Journal of Urban Technology* 20, no. 3 (2013): 65–84.

14 Darren Palmer & Ian Warren, "Surveillance Technology and Territorial Controls: Governance and the 'Lite Touch' of Privacy," *Novatica* (2013): 26–31.

15 Rodrigo Firmino and Fábio Duarte, "Private Video Monitoring of Public Spaces: The Construction of New Invisible Territories," *Urban Studies*, published online (2015): 1–14.

16 It is important to note that, differently to Canada, USA and UK, in Brazil there is no legal or planning equivalent to the figures of Business Improvement Districts (BID) and other similar urban management strategies where businesses and private groups are made legally responsible for a delimited area of the city and, as such, must provide services that are supplemental to those already provided by the municipality, among which surveillance and security. In Brazil, the state is the sole responsible for security in public spaces, sharing responsibilities among its own different levels (local, regional or national governmental bodies).

17 Firmino and Duarte, "Private Video Monitoring of Public Spaces: The Construction of New Invisible Territories".

18 Rem Koolhaas, "My Thoughts on the Smart City," http://ec.europa.eu/archives/commission_2010-2014/kroes/en/content/my-thoughts-smart-city-rem-koolhaas.html (accessed February 10, 2015).

Acknowledgements
The author would like to thank Fábio Duarte for the valuable comments provided during the initial construction of this essay. This work was supported by CNPq (Conselho Nacional de Desenvolvimento Científico e Tecnológico, Ministry of Science, Technology and Innovation, Brazil).

HASAN ELAHI   THOUSAND

Hasan Elahi is an interdisciplinary artist working with issues in surveillance, privacy, migration, citizenship, and the challenges of borders. Elahi's work has been presented in numerous exhibitions at venues such as Centre Georges Pompidou, SITE Santa Fe, the Sundance Film Festival, and the Venice Biennale. Currently, he is an Associate Professor of art at the University of Maryland, roughly equidistant from the headquarters of the CIA, the FBI, and the NSA.

+ VISUAL ARTS, TECHNOLOGY

After having endured a six-month-long FBI investigation in 2002 prompted by an anonymous tip falsely linking him to terrorist activities, Baltimore-based artist Hasan Elahi launched his self-surveillance project *Tracking Transience*. Having begun with emailing photos and information weekly to FBI officers, Elahi soon graduated to a purpose-built website that records his exact physical location (via the GPS system in his mobile phone) allowing the FBI—and everyone else— to constantly monitor his whereabouts. Also recorded on the website is a growing archive of over 70,000 images showing day-to-day details and events from his life: the toilet he used at the airport, the meal he ordered for lunch, the hotel room he stayed in, and even screenshots of financial information and communications. As he noted in a 2011 article in *The New York Times*:

> In an era in which everything is archived and tracked, the best way to maintain privacy may be to give it up. Restricted access to information is what makes it valuable. If I cut out the middleman and flood the market with my information, the intelligence the FBI has on me will be of no value. Making my private information public devalues the currency of the information the intelligence gatherers have collected.

Though Elahi's website is flooded with images and information, one ultimately feels that very little of the artist's life is revealed. Perhaps this is because the artist himself is never pictured in context. *Tracking Transience* is a record of a life in extreme detail, but the detail is mundane and often unremarkable.

Shown here is a detail of the artwork *Thousand Little Brothers* (2014), which appears in full on the next page. The full image is a composition of roughly 32,000 photographs taken from the archives.

STEPHEN GRAHAM
COUNTERGEOGRAPHIES

Stephen Graham is Professor of Cities and Society at Newcastle University's School of Architecture, Planning and Landscape. He has an interdisciplinary background linking human geography, urbanism, and the sociology of technology, which he uses to explore the political aspects of infrastructure, mobility, digital media, surveillance, security, and militarism emphasizing, in particular, how these work to shape contemporary cities and urban life. His books include *Splintering Urbanism* (with Simon Marvin, 2001), *Disrupted Cities: When Infrastructures Fail* (2009), *Cities Under Siege: The New Military Urbanism* (2011) and *Infrastructural Lives* (with Colin McFarlane, 2014).

+ GEOGRAPHY, POLITICS, URBAN STUDIES, VISUAL ARTS

"It's time to draw new maps."[1]

What I refer to as "the new military urbanism"[2] is characterized by a normalized separation of 'us' and 'them'; crumbling market fundamentalism; permanent securocratic war and ubiquitous bordering; accumulation through dispossession; a blurring of the military, entertainment, and security industries; and the mobilization of states of emergency and exception. My question in this context is how might 'countergeographies' be mobilized to contest and disrupt the circuits and logics of this new military urbanism?

Within civil society, especially the multiple media circuits circling the globe, there has been much recent experimentation to address this question. Though scattered and often ephemeral, these experiments present an important complement to more traditional methods of resistance and political mobilization – street protests, social movements, grassroots organizations, and formal political organizing aimed at, for instance, the re-regulation of economies or the redirection of state power.

In these times of war and empire, the idea of the 'public domain' must move beyond the traditional notion that it encompasses media content and geographical space exempt from proprietary control, which combine to "form our common aesthetic, cultural and intellectual landscape."[3] Public domains in contemporary transnational urban life are continually emergent, highly fluid, pluralized, and organized by interactions among many producers and consumers. The new public domains through which countergeographies can be sustained must forge collaborations and connections across distance and difference. Though that's a tall order, requiring extremely strong political and cultural mobilizations which are not currently in evidence, I propose six overlapping avenues of countergeographic experimentation that could help pave the way.

Exposure

First, and most obviously, countergeographies must work to render the invisible visible: to map, visualize, and represent the hidden geographies of the new military urbanism. The task of exposure must confront the fact that the new military urbanism relies on violence to obfuscate what is often taboo or invisible. Once the hidden is unhidden, its seductive and ubiquitous mythologies can be confronted and potentially reversed.[4]

Some excellent work is already emerging on the geographies of commodity chains, on the new international divisions of labor, on offshore services, as well as on questions of resource wars, the dumping of waste, biofuels, biopiracy, the militarization of immigration controls, the global financial crisis, genetically modified crops, and the global construction of agribusiness agriculture. Simply mapping the militarization of borders, and the resulting deaths of 'illegal' immigrants, is a powerful example of this work. Another is addressing the totally different experiences of borders for elites and underclasses, under a state of securocratic war. Italian architect Stefano Boeri, for example, videoed two different journeys within the militarized West Bank, between the same two cities: one journey, rapid and privileged, took place along a Jewish-only highway; the other through the interminable delays, immobility and humiliations of the Israeli check-point system imposed on Palestinians.[5]

An especially productive area of new work is the use of complex graphic design and 'cognitive mapping' to visually capture the dynamics of transnational neoliberalism and militarism. Ashley Hunt's startling *New World Map: In Which We See*—a state-of-the-art visualization of global circuits of neoliberal restructuring, exploitation, social polarization, incarceration and militarization—is an example.[6] The French collective Bureau d'Études has also published a series of brilliant cognitive maps that capture the elite political, economic, technological, and military institutions, which jointly orchestrate neoliberal capitalism. *Infowar/Psychic War*, for example, maps the concentration of control and privatization in transnational corporate media, and links it to doctrines of information warfare. The maps by Bureau d'Études present "an excess of information, demanding a new gaze on the world that we really live in."[7] In so doing, they help reveal the abstract and usually invisible architectures of power that operate beyond democratic control and scrutiny as state, corporate, security, and military players cross-fertilize across global circuits of neoliberal governance.

In this way, cities might become much more than verticalized targets viewed on maps, feral trouble spots within geopolitical abstractions, stylized videoscapes where murderous rampage is presented as entertainment. Instead, they might emerge as fully lived places, seen and inhabited from the ground rather than through the distancing gaze of the video targeting screen, satellite imaging device, geopolitical map, or games console. In the process, the bodies and voices of the living, as well as the bodies of the dead might be made central to the frame.

Juxtaposition

Though simple, juxtaposition is an extremely effective way to bring renderings of 'them' or the 'Other' that help manufacture enmity and war and legitimize state killing into the domestic spaces at the metropolitan cores of power where 'we' live. Juxtaposition aims to debunk the binaries of the Manichaean geographical imagination, and asserts that targeted cities are not demonic or abstract spaces of enmity but lived, embodied civil worlds much like the urban places inhabited by Westerners.

Cartographic juxtaposition offers considerable potential for the subversion of the binaried geographies that sustain the War on Terror. Most influential has been the *You Are Not Here* project, an "urban tourism mash-up" supplying maps of New York and Tel Aviv coordinated with maps of Baghdad and Gaza City. Detailed information about sites in Baghdad and Gaza where war has actually been experienced are delivered, via mobile phone, to people touring New York and Tel Aviv. "Through investigation, local pedestrians are transformed into tourists of foreign places."[8] It becomes possible, when navigating the 'homeland' city, to be vicariously and imaginatively present within the 'enemy' city.

Another fine example of artistic juxtaposition is Paula Levine's *Shadows From Another Place: Baghdad < – > San Francisco* project, which superimposed maps and satellite images of the two cities as the 2003 invasion rolled into Iraq.[9] Bombing attacks on Baghdad by US warplanes during the first wave of Shock and Awe were transposed though GPS coordinates onto equivalent sites in San Francisco. Each site 'hit' in San Francisco was then physically furnished with a container that held information about Levine's project and a list of the latest war dead within the US military.

Levine's Web- and GPS-based maps were set up to help viewers "imagine the impact of political or cultural changes taking place in one location upon another." They worked by "shadowing distant events, overlaying the impact of political and cultural traumas, such as wars or shifts in borders or boundaries, upon local landscapes." In the process, Levine aimed to collapse the binaries of "foreign" and "domestic," to "bridge local and global," and to "allow walkers/viewers to experience spatial and narrative contiguity between separate and distant locations."[10]

Appropriation

A third strategy for the building of countergeographies involves the appropriation and reverse engineering of the very technologies of control that are so central to the new military urbanism. With the eroticization of military control, simulation, and targeting technologies now interwoven through the cultures of leisure, play, consumption, mobility, and tourism, this is an especially important question.

The emphasis here is first to demystify and make visible the invisible technologies of control, tracking, and surveillance that now thoroughly permeate everyday objects, environments, and infrastructures, and then to redeploy them in counter-hegemonic ways. The aim of these experiments is to take apart

the architectures of technology and control so that they can be creatively remodeled and redeployed.

Chris Csikszentmihalyi of MIT, for example, has built a reverse-engineered, unmanned roaming vehicle ("Afghan Explorer") to be deployed to the killing zones of the War on Terror to act as global witness and to overcome restrictions on the press. This vehicle is an "autonomous robot for remote cruising and imaging of rural and urban geopolitical hotspots to gather news for the public in the face of Pentagon press controls of war zones."[11]

In Austria, meanwhile, the System-Civil Counter-Reconnaissance group, led by artist Marko Peljhan, has reverse-engineered military surveillance drones and built their own drone system using a vehicle bought off the Internet.[12] Its task, they say, is a form of countersurveillance – it will work as a "tactical urban countersurveillance system [to] monitor public space."[13] The drone could perhaps enable civil protest groups to protect themselves from violence and other abuses by the state, because they can summon independent media testimony to events in question.

Jamming

Fourth, we need to see widespread efforts to 'jam' the new military urbanism by problematizing and undermining its performances, spectacles, circuits, rituals, and obfuscations. These efforts must address not only the sites of military recruitment, militarizing education, and militarized simulation/entertainment, but also the sites where armaments and control technologies are developed and produced.

For example, Karen Fiorito's 2005 "Shox News Channel: We Distort, You Comply" billboard campaign on Sepulveda Boulevard in Santa Monica, California drew public attention to the convergence of military information operations and supine corporate media—notably News Corporation's Fox News—in sustaining the War on Terror. Another jammer artist, Micah Ian Wright, has reworked a wide range of US World War II-style propaganda posters to hammer home powerful messages about the War on Terror. Among the topics he addresses are the links between SUV use and imperial aggression; the post-9/11 surveillance surge; corporate war-profiteering; the robotization of killing; and the establishment of extra-territorial torture camps.[14]

Jamming is also a relevant response to the efforts of radical Islamists to breed fear and anxiety. The "We're Not Afraid" group, for example, has launched campaigns in various cities targeted by such attacks, as a means both of resisting these attacks and resisting the cycles of securitization they generate. Stressing a strong sense of global cosmopolitanism, rooted in cities, the campaign's message is that "we who are not afraid will continue

1 See noborder.org/nolager.

2 For a fuller account see Stephen Graham, *Cities Under Siege: The New Military Urbanism* (London: Verso, 2010).

3 Patricia Zimmermann, "Public Domains: Engaging Iraq Through Experimental Digitalities," *Framework: The Journal of Cinema and Media* 48, no. 2 (2007): 66-83.

4 Ironically, the mass circulation of digital imaging technologies can bring unintended effects that can do much to expose the new military urbanism's violence. The most powerful acts of exposure are now often inadvertent, caused by leaks from the practitioners of war themselves. The infamous Abu Ghraib torture photos which so de-legitimatized the War on Terror, were, as Patrick Deer reminds us, "produced by the guards themselves as a kind of war-porn designed to document their own everyday lives, as screen savers, as amateur reality TV or a horrifying mutation of *America's Funniest Home Videos*." Patrick Deer, *The Ends of War* (Durham: Duke University Press, 2007) 5.

5 Stefano Boeri, "Solid Sea 03: The Road Map of Multiplicity" (2003), http://www.attitudes.ch/expos/multiplicity/road%20map_gb.htm.

to live our lives the best way we know how. We will work, we will play, we will laugh, we will live. We will not waste one moment, nor sacrifice one bit of our freedom, because of fear."[15]

Satire

Subverting militarization and neoliberalization through satire is part of a long tradition and offers rich possibilities. Inherently moralizing, such interventions are especially successful at exposing the pretensions and absurdities of power and authority. The Yes Men, for example, engage in what they call "identity correction." One or another of them has successfully passed themselves off as corporate or WTO spokesmen, appearing on BBC and other news channels, as a way of inducing "tactical embarrassment" and highlighting the excesses of military and corporate corruption and violence.[16]

In 2004, in the wake of global outrage at the newly circulating pictures of torture at Abu Ghraib prison, a street artist with the pseudonym "Copper Greene" placed adverts mocking Apple's ubiquitous efforts to market its latest generation of iPods on the streets of LA and New York. Among the three images used in the ads is the infamous silhouette of the hooded Iraqi prisoner undergoing "mock electrocution" at Abu Ghraib. Echoing the strapline on the iPod ad, the message reads, "iRaq – 10,000 volts in your pocket, guilty or innocent."

Perhaps the bravest satirical effort, though, must be the work of Danish artist Jakob Boeskov and his pseudo arms company, Empire North. In 2002 Boeskov managed to worm his way into the first major arms and security fair in China to display a product called ID Sniper™. Next to the 'weapon' at the unmanned stall was a poster explaining its purpose:

> What is the ID Sniper™ rifle? It is used to implant a GPS-microchip in the body of a human being, using a high powered sniper rifle as the long distance injector...At the same time, a digital camcorder with a zoom lens fitted within the scope will take a high-resolution picture of the target. ... GPS microchip technology is already being used for tracking millions of pets in various countries, and the logical solution is to use it on humans as well.[17]

By satirizing the obsession to saturate the mass and flux of urban life with the means to identify and track human targets, the ID Sniper™ goes straight to the heart of the technophilic fantasies that drive the new military urbanism. That the Empire North display was accepted as normal within the context of the fair is telling indeed. One computer magazine ran an in-depth article about the Sniper, a delegate tried to purchase the product, and a Chinese company apparently offered venture capital and a manufacturing location to Empire North during the event. As Brian Holmes suggests, what is disturbing is the very ease with which "such invasive technologies are accepted and made into norms. Under these conditions, the work of an artist like Boeskov becomes a rare chance to actually play the governance game, by opening up

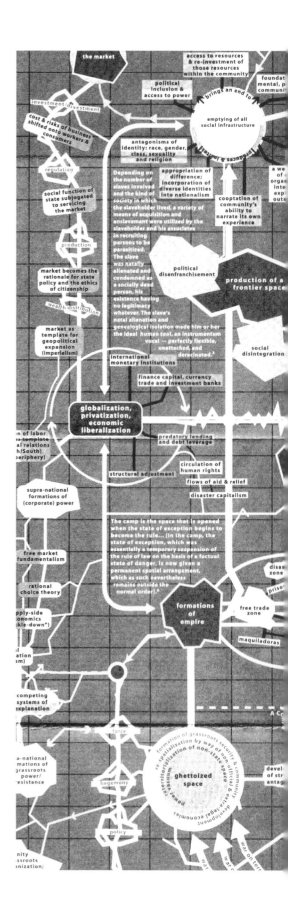

Above: "A World Map: In Which We See" by Ashley Hunt (2007).

a public space for refusing, contesting and challenging these new tracking and recording regimes."[18]

Collaboration

Finally, and perhaps most importantly, countergeographic strategies that attempt to undermine the new military urbanism must work beyond new assertions of cosmopolitanism or democracy. They must engage and collaborate with, rather than merely speaking on behalf of, those on the receiving end of urbicidal violence, the ruthless imposition of neoliberal fundamentalism, and the spread of mass incarceration.

It is necessary to work against the habitual silencing of the non-Western Other because such acts of silencing are often combined with representations that legitimatize the power to penetrate and re-order societies en masse, from afar.[19] Bringing visibility to the non-Western voice and acknowledging the agency of the Other are means of counteracting the tendency to deny non-Western societies what David Slater calls "the legitimate symbols of independent identity and authority" – a tendency that allows the act of representation "to be frozen around the negative attributes of lack, backwardness, inertia and violence."[20]

Where next?

The countergeographies discussed above can each play a part in exposing, debunking or eroding the entrenchment of the new military urbanism around the globe. Perhaps most important, though, the new anti-military urbanism demonstrates that there is an urgent need for radical new concepts of 'security,' capable of serving as the conceptual basis of countergeographies.

To be meaningful for our own time, new concepts of security must forcefully reject traditional notions of national security. The language of security and humanitarianism has all too often cloaked killing, plunder, and dispossession, while complexes of military, corporate, agribusiness, technological, academic, and/ or petrochemical capital have generated massive insecurity at home and abroad. To reimagine security makes it possible to remodel the relation between difference and globalization so that it does not depend on launching boundless and perpetual colonial war against continually targeted Others within and through architectures of hyper-inequality. Huge challenges await, but the starting-points are clear.

First, we must stress the legitimacy and the urgency of countergeographies as powerful means of challenging the legitimacy of violent, fundamentalist ideologies of resistance. "A non-orthodox, non-nostalgic, non-rejectionist, non-apocalyptic critique of the modern," write the Retort collective, "that ought now to be the task of Left politics."[21]

Second, state provision and control must no longer be anathema. We must see to it that socialized infrastructure, housing, and urbanism once again become axiomatic within a resurgent conception of Keynesian state politics, organized through multiple scales of intervention to match the contexts of accelerating globalization.

Third, neoliberal economics must go – *in toto*.

Fourth, progressive redistribution, social and environmental justice, a positive politics of diversity, an idea of difference which resists being violently transposed into otherness – these must become foundational concepts rather than political dirty words confined to the political margins.

Finally, the temporal horizons of politics must reach well beyond the speculative advantages of the 'long now.' Consider, after all, that the human shaping of the earth has become so dominant that an entirely new geological era—the Anthropocene—has been introduced to address it. With fossil-fuel extinction looming, and water and food security rapidly deteriorating, a radical new politics of security requires an appreciation of the demographic pressures and the insecurities created by extreme social polarization, and a grasp of the fact that such polarization is an inevitable hallmark of societies founded on market fundamentalism.

A cautionary note, however. Though they illustrate the breadth of emergent possibilities, the countergeographic initiatives discussed above have very real limitations. Virtually all the initiatives explored here confine themselves to the circuits of artists and activists, and do not cohere into the kind of broader political coalitions necessary to the forging of concerted political challenges. Most claim to speak on behalf of those who bear the brunt, at the receiving end, of the new military urbanism, rather than collaborating with these receivers and their own resistances. But I suggest that if we can encompass the plethora of activist projects within broader political coalitions and movements, then insurgent styles of activism and citizenship would gain the power to make higher-level political demands, thus increasing the possibility that radical ideas of security may be implemented to a meaningful degree.

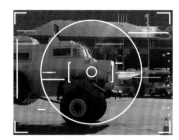
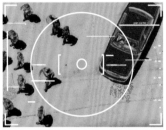

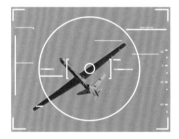

6 Ashley Hunt, "*New World Map: In Which We See*" in Lize Mogel & Alexis Bhagat [eds], *An Atlas of Radical Cartography* [Los Angeles: The Journal of Aesthetics and Protest Press, 2011].

7 Brian Holmes, "Maps for the Outside: Bureau d'Études, or the Revenge of the Concept," message board post, *InterActivist Info Exchange*, available at info.interactivist.net/node/2398.

8 See, youarenothere.org.

9 See, shadowsfromanotherplace.net.

10 Ibid.

11 Zimmerman, "Public Domains."

12 See s-77ccr.org.

13 Ibid.

14 See ministryofhomelandsecurity.blogspot.com.

15 Cited in Cynthia Weber, "An Aesthetics of Fear: The 7/7 London Bombings, the Sublime, and Werenotafraid.com," *Millennium: Journal of International Studies* 34, no. 3 [2006]. See also www.werenotafraid.com.

16 See Stephen Wright, "Spy Art: Infiltrating the Real," *Afterimage* 34, no.1–2 [2006].

17 See www.backfire.dk/empirenorth.

18 Brian Holmes, "Signals, Statistics and Social Experiments: The Governance Conflicts of Electornic Media Art," http://org.noemalab.eu/sections/ideas/ideas_articles/pdf/holmes_signal_statistics.pdf.

19 Denying the Other a voice leads directly to conceiving of the global South as an abstract or pathological 'space ready to be penetrated, worked over, restructured and transformed' from afar, using the superior military or technological power of the West. David Slater, *Geopolitics and the Post-Colonial: Rethinking North-South Relations* [London: Blackwell, 2004], 222.

20 Ibid.

21 Retort, *Afflicted Powers: Capital and Spectacle in a New Age of War* [London: Verso, 2004], 177.

Note:
This paper is an edited and condensed version of the concluding chapter of *Cities Under Siege: The New Military Urbanism* [London: Verso, 2010]. The paper was adapted for publication by the LA+ Journal editorial team with the express permission of the author.

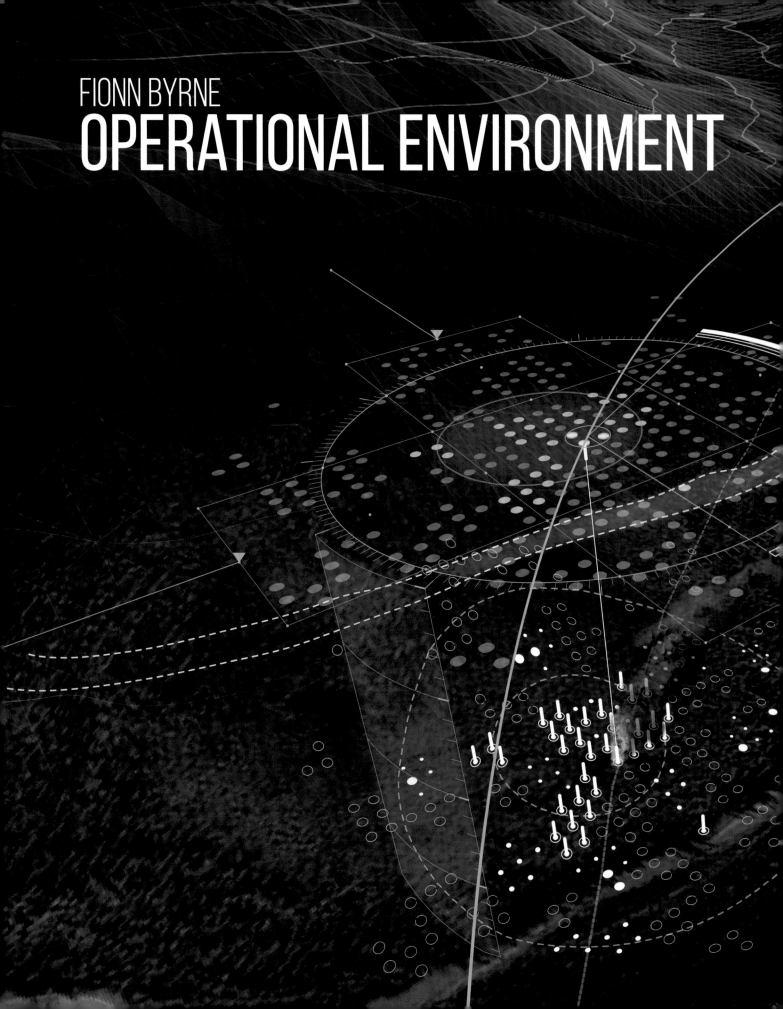

FIONN BYRNE
OPERATIONAL ENVIRONMENT

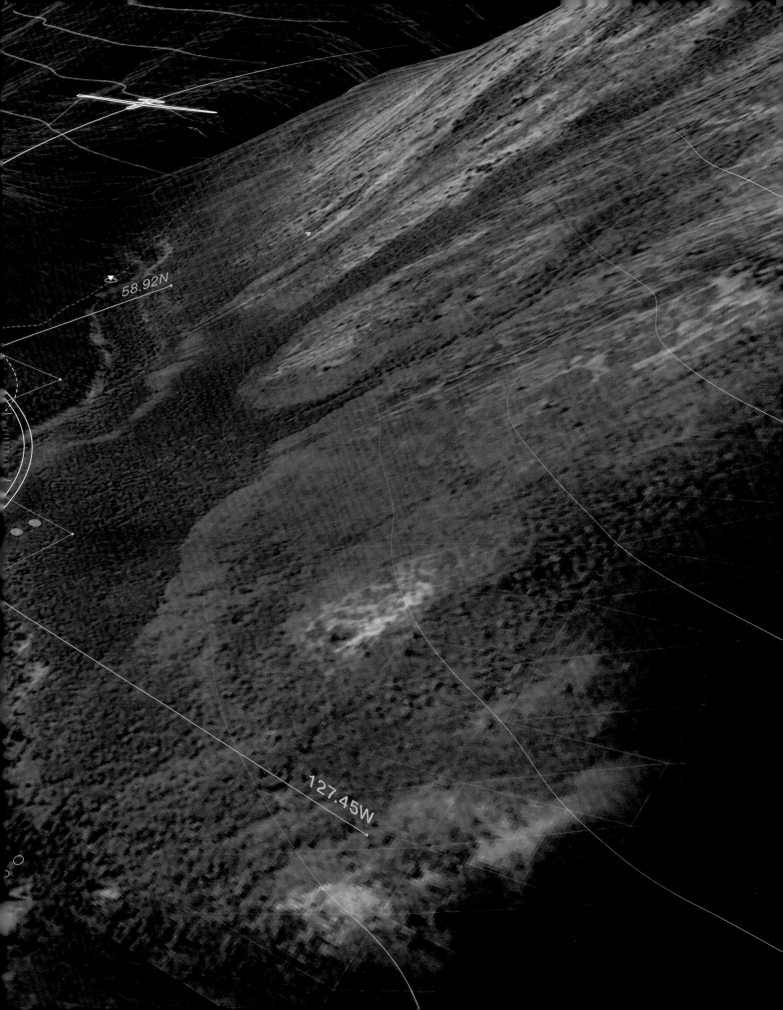

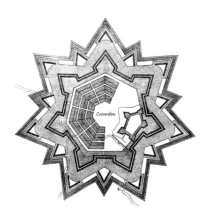

Fionn Byrne is a landscape architect and lecturer at Harvard University's Graduate School of Design where he holds the 2015–2016 Daniel Urban Kiley Teaching Fellowship in Landscape Architecture. Byrne has also taught at the University of Toronto and the University of Waterloo. His work can be found online at pedonicoperations.com.

✚ MILITARY STRATEGY, REGIONAL PLANNING, MAPPING

Above: 1647 star fortification plan for the city Coevorden in the Netherlands.

Opposite: Mission briefing of the 99th Bombardment Group aircrews, Foggia, Italy, 1944.

Associations between landscape architecture and the military industrial complex throughout history and to this day should be familiar and well documented, but they are not. And yet, the military and landscape architecture share similar methods and technologies, even if purposed for different ends. This essay attempts to expose several "cords of militariality"[1] that bind the profession of landscape architecture to a conceptual and physical militarization of the environment. This is potentially an important relationship to explore both in theory and practice as the planet is increasingly defined in both military *and* ecological terms.

While landscape architects will be familiar with the work of André Le Nôtre and the ways in which the mathematics of ballistics influenced the design of the gardens of Versailles,[2] discussed less frequently is the work of Sébastien Le Prestre de Vauban,[3] a military engineer who constructed star fortifications. His work perfected techniques of manipulating the ground plane to allow or deny views; however, in this case view-sheds corresponded to projectile trajectories and thus defending or taking life.[4] In both cases topography was transformed into a static condition mathematically optimized to guarantee effectiveness. The star fort was primarily a defensive structure designed in anticipation of predictable future aggression,[5] and so there was time to perfect the construction without being under direct threat. This method of military action as precise control of static topographic conditions corresponding to optics, or more specifically to ballistic trajectories, is paralleled in landscape works where the biophysical environment is treated in the same way. Both military engineers and landscape architects constructed precise topographic manipulations with the same reliance on geometry and optics.[6]

Another example of connections between landscape architecture and the military is the rise in prevalence and importance of aerial imaging in the mid-20th century. A growing body of literature substantiates a relationship between advances in military aerial technologies for visualizing the planet's surface and a subsequent rise in the popularity of landscape ecology, planning, and design.[7] Carl Troll and Ian McHarg are two central figures in this discussion, and most landscape architects will have some familiarity with their work and legacy. Advances in military technology, research, and methods often provide benefits to civilian professions outside of wartime operations, and landscape architecture is no exception. In *Flights of Imagination: Aviation, Landscape, Design*, Sonja Dümpelmann reminds us that Carl Troll returned to Germany in the 1930s with the aim of securing geographical photographic research as critically relevant to warfare. Troll worked during World War II to demonstrate how his method could have practical applications to the success of military campaigns and after the war applied this same methodology and use of technology to questions of urban planning and ecological science.[8] McHarg also served during World War II and while less outspoken than Troll it is clear that his overlay analysis is indebted in part to advances in German and American mapping, data visualization, and geographic technologies.[9] In the same way, the establishment of the Environmental Systems Research Institute (Esri) by Jack Dangermond would be difficult

to imagine without wartime advances in Geographic Information Systems (GIS). The legacy of this historic alignment is with us today, as landscape architects are most often found initiating projects with an aerial understanding of site and the landscape overlay method introduced by McHarg has now become standard procedure in landscape architecture.[10] Of course, as Charles Waldheim has warned, the danger is that aerial imaging indiscriminately reduces the environment to "quantifiable data in a global economy of information,"[11] and, when so reduced, this data is accumulated by the modern military in its quest for control of information.[12]

Indeed, it seems military dominance is now predicated on a technological superiority of accumulating spatial environmental information.[13] This belief, irrespective of whether true or false, has legitimized the expansion of the technological architecture of the US military to develop persistent means of imaging, measuring, and visualizing the entire globe in anticipation of future military engagements.[14] In so doing, the diversity of the earth's ecosystem and all life is necessarily reduced to "identifiable self-present identities" easily categorized and defined as potential targets.[15] In conjunction to this, there is a growing acceptance of characterizing the biophysical nature of the planet as at risk and in need of intervention. Climate change casts the environment as both threatened and as a threat.[16] In this way, the language of terror and security is extended beyond the urban physical environment without geographic restriction. The ecological crisis of climate

1 Robert P. Marzec, "Militariality," *The Global South* 3, no. 1 (2009): 147.

2 Patricia Bouchenot-Déchin & Georges Farhat, *André Le Nôtre in Perspective* (Paris: Editions Hazan, 2014), 175.

3 The relationship between André Le Nôtre and Sébastien Le Prestre de Vauban in another essay could similarly be compared to Federick Law Olmsted and Egbert Viele, the West Point–trained military engineer who drafted accurate topographic and drainage plans as well as geological sections all prior to Vaux and Olmstead's competition entry. See, for example, Morrison H. Heckscher, *Creating Central Park* (Metropolitan Museum of Art, 2008): 15–19.

4 John Muller, *A Treatise Containing the Elementary Part of Fortification, Regular and Irregular* (Ottawa: Museum Restoration Service, 1968).

5 Burton Wright III, "A Genius for Fortification: Vauban and the Future of Positional Warfare," *Engineer* 30, no. 2 (2000): 37–39.

Above: The environment in military terms is now transformed from a theater in which to wage war to being itself an operational target.

change is poised to extend the state of emergency enacted by the American government since 9/11, and to become both universal and permanent.[17] The normalization of this condition will put in place a framework within which any threat to global capitalism and national sovereignty shall be defined as of military concern and a target for pre-emptive action and control.[18] Global warming by human-induced climatic change thus sets the environment to be defined as either recalcitrant in its commitment to supplying resources or, worse yet, to be defined as an aggressor, within a paradigm of terrorism, for its ongoing deployment of natural disasters.

This combination of an unrelenting 'informationalizing' and projective management has transformed the environment in military terms from being a theater in which to wage war to being itself an operational target. As both a subject of passive study and active modification, the force of the military's technological, informational, and industrial apparatus is being set upon the environment, reducing nature to both a resource as standing reserve on the one hand and a technological-controlled, environmentally managed set of ecosystems on the other.[19] It is Heidegger's notion of "standing reserve," the systematic ordering

of nature as a potential resource according to a technological enframing,[20] that is the basis of Waldheim's earlier warning of the power of aerial imaging to reduce the environment to valuated data. This is not a hypothetical or abstract conceptualization of the environment, but a very real redefinition of our relationship to nature that stands ready to obviate the possibility of any nature exterior to or sovereign from human observation, control, and valuation as resource.

What should be regarded by landscape architects as a particularly worrying example of this way of thinking is the banality of the design recommendations that come towards the conclusion of Simon Dalby's book *Security and Environmental Change*. Using a language that seems borrowed directly from Richard T.T. Forman, Dalby states:

> Habitats are key to maintaining ecological diversity and essential to the health of any species... But habitats need to be interconnected so that animals, birds, and plants can move and adapt to changing circumstances. Artificial linear barriers like roads, and aerial barriers like cities and fields, dangerously compromise mobility for many species.[21]

The point is not that Dalby is appropriating an ecological vocabulary towards suspicious or malicious ends (in fact, he uses ecological adaptation to environmental change as a metaphor to critique the security paradigm of stability),[22] but rather that his writing is outside the consciousness of landscape theory and practice, as is a growing body of work in cultural studies and philosophy, not to mention political ecology, environmental security, and others who are more conscious of the important connections being made between the military, environmental theory, and politics.

As the environment becomes increasingly subsumed into military affairs, landscape architects are poised to either facilitate or challenge the militarization of the globe. As a profession that works best through interdisciplinary relationships, we have a unique ability to dialogue with engineers, ecologists, cultural theorists, the public, and the military. The profession's familiarity with mapping and analysis, the understanding of economy and ecology as science and politics, and practice of planning infrastructure and urbanism situates us as potentially integral to the success of the military's campaign against climate change. Reciprocally, landscape architecture could be rewarded with greater power, not to mention part of the US Department of Defense's (FY 2014) base budget of $526.6 billion in discretionary funding.[23]

And yet, at the same time, the profession is positioned to question the militarization of the environment in several ways. For example, we can question first the logic of adaptation to climate change instead of seeking alternative modes of living that do not transform the environment in the same way; second, the paradigm of national security by acknowledging that environments are always subject to change and risk; third, the reduction of nature to standing reserve by designing an ecology that denies quantitative performance; and fourth, the characterization of nature as a wild and untamed other that requires control by recognizing nature's 'otherness' is produced in large part by the use of a non-human aerial point of view.

Clearly the brevity of this essay requires that few examples be presented, but there remains much work to be done on documenting the parallel preoccupations of landscape architects and military strategists. Historical alignments can serve to better understand both contemporary practices and allow for projective comments on future relations. While climate change and post-peak resources are today characterizing the environment as a military problem, it is worthwhile to question how military theory comes to understand 'environment' and to use design as a tool to critique developments in the military's technological apparatus for observing, modifying, and controlling the environment.

6 Michel Baridon, *A History of the Gardens of Versailles* (Philadelphia: University of Pennsylvania Press, 2008), 96.

7 Charles Waldheim, "Aerial Representation and the Recovery of Landscape," in James Corner (ed.) *Recovering Landscape* (New York: Princeton Architectural Press, 1999), 121–39; Mike Hill, 7"Ecologies of War," in Tom Cohen (ed.) *Telemorphosis: Theory in the Era of Climate Change, Vol. 1* (Michigan: Open Humanities Press, 2012): 239–69

8 Sonja Dümpelmann, *Flights of Imagination: Aviation, Landscape, Design* (London: University of Virginia Press, 2014): 107.

9 Keith C. Clarke & John G. Cloud, "On the Origins of Analytical Cartography," *Cartography and Geographic Information Science* 27, no. 3 (2000): 197.

10 Christophe Girot, "The Elegance of Topology," in Christophe Girot (ed.) *Topology: topical thoughts on the contemporary landscape* (Berlin: Jovis, 2013), 80. Girot's work, in searching for alternatives to the overlay method, is quite interestingly experimenting with the next generation of military surveillance and mapping technologies: drones and point clouds.

11 Waldheim, "Aerial Representation and the Recovery of Landscape," 133.

12 Robert P. Marzec, "Militariality," *The Global South* 3, no. 1 (2009): 141.

13 M. Christine Boyer, "Urban Operations and Network Centric Warfare," in Michael Sorkin (ed.) *Indefensible Space: The Architecture of the National Insecurity State* (New York: Taylor and Francis, 2008), 52.

14 Ibid.

15 Robert P. Marzec, "Militarized Ecologies: Visualizations of Environmental Struggle in the Brazilian Amazon," *Public Culture* 26, no. 2 (2014): 242.

16 Ibid.

17 Mick Smith, *Against Ecological Sovereignty: Ethics, Biopolitics, and Saving the Natural World* (University of Minnesota Press, 2011), 204.

18 Ibid.

19 Simon Dalby, *Security and Environmental Change* (Cambridge: Polity Press, 2009), 159.

20 Smith, *Against Ecological Sovereignty*, 103.

21 Dalby, *Security and Environmental Change,* 167.

22 Ibid., 4.

23 The White House, "Department of Defense: The Budget for Fiscal Year 2014," http://www.whitehouse.gov/sites/default/files/omb/budget/fy2014/assets/defense.pdf (accessed February 22, 2015).

EMERALD CITY

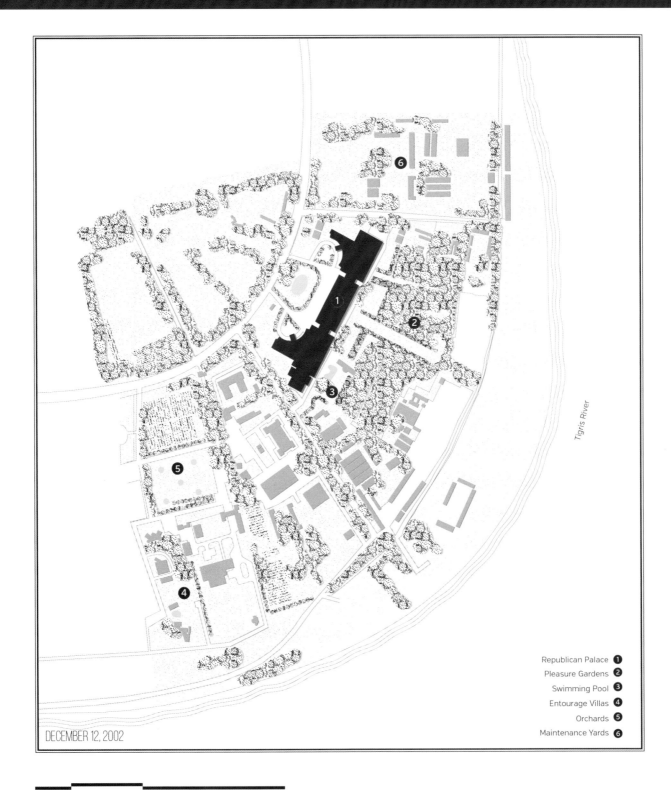

Republican Palace **1**
Pleasure Gardens **2**
Swimming Pool **3**
Entourage Villas **4**
Orchards **5**
Maintenance Yards **6**

DECEMBER 12, 2002

Tigris River

0   250 ft   500 ft   1000 ft

Saddam Hussein built his Republican Palace on the banks of the Tigris River in Baghdad, Iraq, to insulate the center of Iraqi power from the realities of everyday life in the city. After Saddam's removal from power, the Coalition Provisional Authority turned the palace into its headquarters, and the area surrounding the palace became the hub for coalition activity in the region.

From 2003 to 2009, coalition staffers and the private contractors supporting them lived in trailer parks located in Saddam's former pleasure gardens. Despite having removed most of the trees and lawn to accommodate the new infrastructure, the standard of living in the compound was so high in comparison to the rest of Baghdad that it became known as 'The Emerald City.' In 2009 it was rechristened as the Iraq Government Palace and now hosts ceremonial and diplomatic gatherings.

N

Tigris River

CPA Headquarters ❶
'Poolside Estates' (CPA Housing) ❷
Swimming Pool ❸
CPA Motor Pool ❹
Helipad ❺
'Ocean Cliffs' (British Housing) ❻

AUGUST 19, 2004

Sources: Rajiv Chandrasekaran, *Imperial Life in the Emerald City: Inside Iraq's Green Zone* (New York: Alfred A. Knopf, 2006), p. 25; Jane Arraf, "Iraq unveils refurbished palace where US soldiers once hung laundry," *The Christian Science Monitor* (April 11, 2011).

TRAUMA

PATRIZIA VIOLI

SCAPES

THE CASE OF THE 9/11 MEMORIAL

Patrizia Violi is Full Professor of Semiotics at the University of Bologna, Italy. She is also the Director of TRAME: Interdisciplinary Centre for the Study of Memory and Cultural Traumas (www.trame.unibo.it), at the University of Bologna. Her main areas of research include textual analysis, language and gender, and semantic theory, on which themes she has published numerous articles and volumes, including: *Meaning and Experience* (2001). She is currently working on cultural semiotics and traumatic memory, in particular in relation to memorials and memory museums. On the latter theme she recently published *Paesaggi Della Memoria: Il trauma, lo spazio, la storia* (2014).

✛ SEMIOTICS, CULTURAL STUDIES

No other time in history other than the present seems so concerned with the memory of trauma, and no other time seems to have so many memorials and memory museums dedicated to tragic, traumatic collective events. The number of such places has grown exponentially over the last few decades, both in Europe and in the United States, although a more accurate analysis of which traumas appear to be worth memorializing is quite another story. In the United States there are certainly more memorials of the Holocaust—an act of genocide that did not happen in that country—than there are of the genocide of Native Americans, on which the very foundation of the nation itself is grounded.

But what exactly is the role of memorials in terms of constructing, transmitting, and defining a collective memory of the events they claim to commemorate? Which story do they tell, which social functions do they fulfill? These are questions we should ask ourselves when visiting the memorials that are more and more often becoming a part of our urban landscapes. At first sight a memorial appears to be merely a place to 'conserve' and store a memory of some given event. There is first an event, then the decision to remember it, and then the memorial, often resulting from merely maintaining the precise place where the event occurred, thus transforming that space into a place of worship, something between a sacred space and a tourist attraction.

But if we look more closely, things appear less straightforward, and the relationship between event, space, and memory less linear. Rather than just maintaining a record of the past, memorials and monuments actually contribute to its reconstruction in precisely those actual forms and modalities selected for its memorialization. What, at first glance, has appeared to be a pure trace of the past becomes the actual origins of its current meaning. Thus, memorials are not only places of remembrance, they are also places where history becomes rewritten, transformed, sanctified, and sometimes, too, normalized.

If wars are not only carried out on battlefields, but also through the many-faced articulations of war propaganda, history too is not only written through history books, but rather by the numerous and various social narrations that contribute to our perceptions of the past. Historical memory is not something well defined once and for all, but rather something that is changing continuously over time: the actual events themselves are remembered differently, according to the different discourses, texts, images, symbols, and gestures produced in relation to them. Even the Holocaust is not remembered in the same way today as it was 50 years ago, in Germany, in Israel, Poland, or the United States, before or after the well-known *Holocaust* television series of the late 1970s.

Memorials are yet another of those 'texts' that influence our current ways of understanding the meanings of past events, each contributing in its own way to consolidate these according to the actual forms chosen for their material constitution. In this way, they could well be seen as a key element of the cultural stabilization of memorialization processes: their own way of rewriting history becomes what we then perceive as history itself. Memorials and monuments play a crucial role in the actual construction of events, by delimitation of their boundaries and, more than anything else, by their stabilization into new forms that we then come to perceive as 'given'.[1]

It is precisely this form of 'rewriting' that I would like to problematize in relation to the 9/11 Memorial Museum, a very complex site of memory that includes both a Memorial and a Museum – two quite different forms of memorialization in both their aims and functions. Many things have been already written about this place of memory,[2] which has been criticized from both right-wing and left-wing factions, for different, and occasionally opposing, reasons. Indeed, contradictions are bound to permeate a place that is at the same time a mass grave and a vast commercial center, a place of mourning and a tourist attraction. Even the extremely fastidious security apparatus that regulates the entrance– although it might well be indispensable–appears somehow incongruous in a place that is supposed, after all, to celebrate the value of freedom against the cruel blindness of terrorism. One is reminded of the security procedure of an airport check-in, which turned out to be so inefficient in the actual case in question (and indeed in the museum, one can see the displayed security video taken at the airport on the morning of September 11, 2001, where the terrorists can be seen passing through without any problem at all).

In this discussion I focus primarily on the memorial itself, and the ways in which it contributes to defining and 'freezing' the September 11 event. My reason for this choice builds on the fact that the memorial appears to be the real core of the whole Ground Zero memory complex, and that which is most likely to remain imprinted in the hearts and minds of visitors.

The emotional and aesthetic core of the memorial is the two chasms that have been opened up in the very place where the twin towers once stood, two empty holes where the gaze of the visitor dissolves in the endless cycle of the waterfall. The intensity of this place is certainly partly due to the visual effect of water falling into a void and evoking, in a reverse mirror effect, the collapse of the two towers and the almost 3,000 lives lost during the event (as the names inscribed in the borders of the two chasms remind us). But this is only one part of the story. The most powerful aspect of the memorial stems from the *indexical* nature of the two chasms, since this space is precisely where the traumatic event

itself took place. An index, according to American philosopher and semiotician Charles Sanders Peirce,[3] is a sign that exhibits a direct, causal link to the actual event that produced the sign, and which the sign itself, in its turn, signifies. Indexical signs are thus material traces of the past, with direct spatial links to it, and this endows them with a very unique type of meaning effect: the two chasms themselves would be far less powerful if they were not actually situated in exactly the same place as the two foundations of the twin towers.

There also seems to be an especially strong, almost mysterious, connection between death and the actual place of its occurrence, turning it somehow into a sacred space, with a quite unique evocative, and symbolic, power. We feel the need to return there, making it into a place of pilgrimage, bringing flowers to mark it, as is often the case in many countries in the world where small roadside memorials are erected at places where fatal road accidents have taken place.

But where does such need, or perhaps desire, come from? Why do we want to actually "be" in the *same space* where the deadly event happened? I think this might well have something to do with a deep need to share something with the victims, a desire, as Vikki Bell has observed, "to put oneself in the place of the other, not just to understand it from the point of view of the other, but from the very *place* where the other once stood."[4] If so, then indexicality does not only characterize places, but also, in a way, the actual experience of visiting them. *Here* is where the events happened, and it is *here* where we as visitors are now standing and experiencing just being *here*. A similar double indexical anchoring installs a strong link between the present of the actual visit and the past of the event, activating a powerful emphatic participation in it, if not a kind of identification with the victims. We could define the memorial as an *affective architecture* in that it indexes not only the physical space of the event, but also the actual experience of the visitors while being there.

But what exactly is the 'event' that the twin tower chasms commemorate through their anchoring of this particular space to the past? At first sight, the question might seem preposterous: obviously they are there to remember the event of September 11, 2001; that is, the collapse of the towers. The idea that September 11 actually *is* the event, and coincides fully with that actual moment in time, is something so fully assumed that it appears difficult to question it. But is this really the case? Perhaps events are of a more complicated nature, so that they, and their temporal definition, are more open to questioning.

Today, there is a broadly shared understanding that events are not 'natural' phenomena independent of the various ways in which they are reconstructed, narrated, and memorized. According to Robin Wagner-Pacifici, events are restless, unstable entities, complex mobile social processes unbounded in their temporal delimitations.[5] Events are restless because they are continuously being interpreted, framed and reframed by the discourses, images, words, and texts that construct and reconstruct their very meanings, in an endless process of interpretation that reminds us of what Umberto Eco referred to as "unlimited semiosis."[6] In this perspective, events can be seen as "shape-shifters" or "relays of signs and symbols"[7] that can range from treaties to television series, from gestures of condolence to institutional speeches, from images to monuments. This extremely heterogeneous set of semiotic configurations and social narratives constitutes what Aby Warburg once called the "afterlife of events"[8] – an afterlife, I would like to add, that actually has retroactive effects on the events themselves, thus redefining their very nature.

The afterlife of September 11 is certainly one of the most arresting of our time, since this event was the beginning of something new (an infinitely more worrying and destabilizing story than those we were previously used to), the story of our now frightening present apparently opening up for a even more horrendous future. Indeed, as pointed out by Wagner-Pacifici, in the case of September 11 it is no small issue to determine where the event actually begins and where it ends.[9] Is it defined by the moment the twin towers collapsed in New York City? Does it encompass the attack on the Pentagon and the plane crash in Pennsylvania? Is it confined to 9/11 or does it include the days immediately after, with their dramatic search to identify victims? What about the longer-term consequences of an event that in many aspects changed the history of our time, from the Afghanistan and Iraq wars and perhaps up to and including the more recent spreading of terrorist attacks all over the world, the diffusion of ISIS and the apparent increasing militarization of everyday life?

At first sight, all this has little to do with a memorial. We cannot expect a memorial to capture the complexity of an event of this magnitude, or account for the whole chain of events that followed the initial, principal trauma. In a way, we could even say that monuments and memorials are erected precisely to memorialize a given event by fixing it in time, by putting to rest the inherently restless nature of the event, and thus playing a very important role in stabilizing and privileging certain readings of the past over others.

Because, if it is true that events are indeed 'restless,' there are nonetheless, at the same time, forms of retardation and stabilization within this seemingly endless process of production and interpretation of meaning. Semiosis is thus unlimited only in principle: in the reality of historical processes there will always be moments where the process stops, though perhaps only temporarily, and meanings thus become stabilized. Peirce described such moments of inertia and consolidation of meaning as "habit:" a tendency to favor one particular interpretation over all other potential interpretations, and to behave accordingly.[10] We certainly need forms of sedimentation in the dynamic of semiosis, forms of stasis where memories acquire a given shape, though not ever a permanent one. Memorials and museums are generally of one of these forms, commemorations are another.

However, just how memorials might accomplish such a goal is something far from universally recognized, especially when they are situated directly where the traumatic event happened (thus carrying with them a strong indexical link). In these cases memorials encompass physical traces that might appear endowed with an almost natural capacity to bear memories of the past. But it is not that simple: these memorialized traces are always subject to the interpretation of both the designer and the visitor. Over the last few years a very intense debate has taken place all over the world regarding how to conserve, memorize, or transform—that is, how to interpret—what I have defined elsewhere as "trauma sites,"[11] a complex debate which involves not only the architectural design of such sites, but more crucially, the kinds of social and cultural functions they ought to fulfill. In Argentina, for example, a long discussion has developed over the years regarding how to conserve ESMA (*Escuela Superior de Mecánica de la Armada*), a huge military complex in Buenos Aires used previously as a place of imprisonment, torture, and murder by the military.[12] While some associations of survivors and relatives of victims wished to conserve the place exactly as it was, thus maintaining the strong indexical links with the past, other associations, such as the *Madres de Plaza de Mayo*, for example, were in favor of using the place as a youth center. According to the *Madres*, the site should not take the form of a memorial that fixes

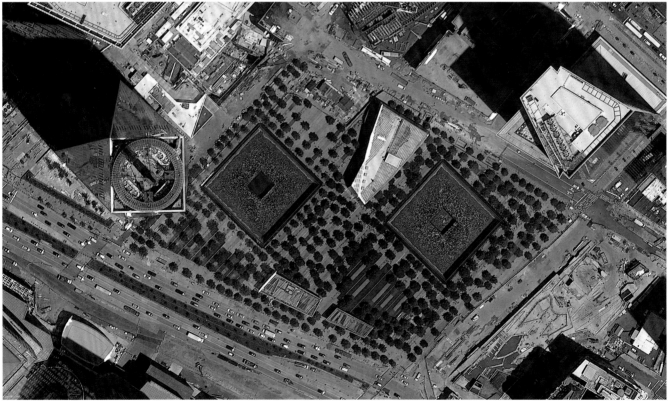

and forecloses the past, but rather one that allows for a new future, by suggesting new forms of social and cultural life.[13] The Argentinean debate shows how the very same traces of the events of the past can be interpreted and redesigned in very different ways.

The 9/11 memorial, with its cyclical and never-ending deluges of water into two stark black holes, evokes the image of the collapse of the two towers, thus freezing the whole event into that very last moment. The particular stabilization of meaning realized by the memorial is focused on the conclusion of the event; using a linguistic terminology we could say that the process is described from a terminative point of view, thus fixing the temporal boundaries of the event so that they coincide precisely with its conclusion. Independently of any consideration of the aesthetic values inherent in the memorial (which is not what I am concerned with here), other realizations would have produced different meaning effects. For example, the two rays of light emanating from the craters and diffusing into the sky, as designed by Libeskind, display a different system of topological oppositions (high instead of low, infinite diffusion instead of eternal circularity), which might easily be seen as opening up for different kinds of memorization.

There is also another aspect that should be taken into account when discussing the form that memorials contribute to commemorating traumatic events. Although memorials and monuments are architectural artifacts that typically do not change over time, they are nevertheless immersed in a living environment, and are, or might be, subject to different kinds of remembrance practices–often unforeseen by their designers–that have a noticeable feedback effect on the perceptions and overall meanings of the monument itself. Such was the case, for example, with Maya Lin's Vietnam Veterans Memorial in Washington, DC. Here, the sober form of the monument was subsequently transformed through spontaneous practices of remembrance and commemoration, as relatives and friends brought flowers, flags, and other small objects to the monument to remember their own loved ones, thus changing the design's overall profile.[14]

Monuments are not isolated objects that merely stand in the void; they are often installed into an urban context that surrounds them and affects our understanding of them, as they become subjected to various kinds of remembrance practices. Within this perspective, it becomes particularly interesting to examine more closely the discussion that took place in late 2010, when a plan was announced to build an Islamic Center two blocks north of Ground Zero. The Islamic Community Center was supposed to include a mosque, a school, a pool, and a 9/11 memorial. Seen at the beginning as uncontroversial, in a few months it became a highly contested project, due to the potential proximity to Ground Zero of a mosque and a center for Islamic culture.[15] The intense debate that followed, where family members of

the victims as well as politicians and residents were involved, showed very well how the actual surroundings of a monument can be sensitive, and that the kinds of activities carried out around a memory place will play a major role in defining the overall sense of that place. Preventing the construction of a mosque nearby emphasized the sacralization of the memorial, freezing it into a time and space that is non-contaminable by other events, actors, or narratives. Moreover, it implicitly set out which religions were to be admitted to this place of memory and which were not, also reflecting somehow on who had the right to claim a legitimate status of victim.

These examples remind us that the meaning of a memorial is not only a matter of its actual design. How we read memorials can change in relation to their environments, and they may acquire different meanings over time, reflecting the various usages and practices carried out there. The ongoing transformation of the Lower Manhattan area may well influence the future functioning of the 9/11 memorial, as well as the different perceptions we have of it. And, in the long run, the surrounding environment may influence the very ways in which we remember the event itself. Memory is part of the event, and not its automatic consequence, so the choices we make regarding forms of memorialization will always have retroactive effects on our ways of thinking about the event itself.

1 See on this point, amongst others: Arnold-De-Simine Silke, *Mediating Memory in the Museum: Trauma, Empathy, Nostalgia* (Houndmills: Palgrave Macmillan, 2013). Patrizia Violi, *Paesaggi della memoria. Il trauma, lo spazio, la storia.* (Milano: Bompiani, 2014). Paul Williams, *Memorial Museums: The Global Rush to Commemorate Atrocities* (Oxford, New York: Berg, 2007).

2 See, amongst others, Adam Gopnik, "Stones and Bones: Visiting the 9/11 memorial and museum," *The New Yorker* (July 7, 2014); Patricia Cohen, "Families continue protest of plan for 9/11 remains," *The New York Times* (March 5, 2012); Patricia Cohen, "Unhealed Wounds Complicate the Choices for 9/11 museum," *The New York Times* (June 17, 2012); David B. Caruso, "World Trade Center Monument: The Future Emerges at Ground Zero," *Buffalo News* (March 20, 2011); David Rief, "After 9/11: The Limits of Remembrance," *Harper's Magazine* 1935 (August 2001): 46–50; Georgina Kay, "The Resilient City: New York after 9/11 and the New WTC designs," in Peter J. M. Nas (ed.), *Cities Full of Symbols: A Theory of Urban Space and Culture* (Leiden: Leiden University Press, 2011), 259–81.

3 C Charles Sanders Peirce, *Collected Papers of Charles Sanders Peirce* (Cambridge: Harvard University Press, 1931), 2.92, 2.247, 2.283, and 4.531.

4 Vikki Bell, *The Art of Post-Dictatorship: Ethics and Aesthetics in Transitional Argentina* (London: Routledge, 2014), 76.

5 Robin Wagner-Pacifici, "Theorizing the Restlessness of Events," *American Journal of Sociology* 115, no. 5 (2010): 1351, 1386.

6 Eco Umberto, *A Theory of Semiotics* (Bloomington: Indiana University Press, 1976), 69.

7 Wagner-Pacifici, "Theorizing the Restlessness of Events," 1366.

8 The word used by Aby Warburg is Nachleben, which is rather difficult to translate into English. It is usually translated as 'afterlife': that should not, however, be understood in the sense of another life beyond the present, but rather as a continued life where the past becomes actual in the present. Warburg Aby, "Die Funktion der nachlebenden Antike bei der Ausprägung energetischer Symbolik" in Aby Warburg, *Gesammelte Schriften, Studienausgabe, vol. II, 2: Bilderreihen und Austellungen,* Uwe Fleckern & Isanella Woldt (eds), (Berlin: Akademie Verlag, [1927] 2012), 115–33.

9 Wagner-Pacifici Robin, "Theorizing the Restlessness of Events," *American Journal of Sociology* 115, No. 5 (2010): 1351.

10 Peirce, *Collected Papers of Charles Sanders Peirce*, 5.397–8.

11 Patrizia Violi, "Trauma Site Museums and Politics of Memory: Tuol Sleng, Villa Grimaldi and Bologna Ustica Museum," *Theory Culture & Society* 29, no. 1 (2012): 36-75.

12 Marcelo Brodsky (ed.), *Memoria en construción. El debate sobre ESMA* (Buenos Aires: La Marca, 2005).

13 Ibid.

14 Robin Wagner-Pacifici & Barry Schwartz, "The Vietnam Veterans memorial: Commemorating a Difficult Past," *American Journal of Sociology* 97, no. 2 (1991): 376–420.

15 See, on this point, Fareed Zakaria, "The real ground zero: let's promote Muslim moderates right here," *Newsweek* (2010, August 16), 19; Lisa Miller, "War over ground zero: a proposed mosque tests the limits of American tolerance," *Newsweek* (2010, August 16), 27–33; Andrea Peyser, "Mosque madness at ground zero," *New York Post* (2010, May 13).

TREES AND MEMORY IN RWANDA

NICHOLAS PEVZNER

Nicholas Pevzner is a full-time lecturer in the Department of Landscape Architecture at the University of Pennsylvania School of Design, and is Co-Editor-in-Chief of *Scenario Journal*, an online publication devoted to showcasing and facilitating the emerging interdisciplinary conversation between landscape architecture, urban design, engineering, and ecology. Prior to joining the UPenn faculty, he was a designer at the landscape architecture firm Michael Van Valkenburgh Associates in New York. He holds an undergraduate degree in architecture and a master's degree in landscape architecture.

✚ ETHNOGRAPHY, CULTURAL GEOGRAPHY, POLITICS,
LANDSCAPE ECOLOGY

Acknowledgements
Thanks to Katherine Klein and Randall Mason for organizing travel and contacts in Rwanda as part of their ongoing work on the Ntarama Genocide Memorial. Thanks also to Issa Higiroi and Ernest Mutwarasibo whose insightful observations helped me to glimpse the cultural landscape of Bugesera through Rwandan eyes.

Some countries become famous for their landscapes, their cuisine, or their national monuments: Rwanda became famous for its gorillas and its genocide. Over just 100 days in the spring of 1994, at least 800,000 Rwandans were killed by their neighbors and countrymen.[1] Today, the signs of mass murder are long gone; although bodies are still occasionally found, most of the victims' remains have been collected and concentrated at a handful of memorial sites around the country. There certainly is little evidence of the inconceivably horrific bloodletting in the lush green landscape just outside Kigali. The landscape seems the epitome of efficient, orderly land use and peaceful agrarian existence. But to the initiated, the trees in Rwanda represent a layer of the landscape that is intimately tied to the history of social upheaval, of genocide, as well as to the history of national reconciliation and rebirth. One just has to know where to look.

The neat agricultural scenes belie the extent to which this landscape has been controlled and shaped by the intense pressure of population: whereas at the turn of the 20th century Rwanda still had 30% of its original forests, by 1997 only 7% remained.[2] Rwanda's population increased fourfold between 1948 and 1993[3] to become Africa's most densely populated country; in an economy where agriculture accounts for the livelihoods of nine out of 10 people, the intense competition for land was undoubtedly one of the factors that set the stage for conflict. Today the countryside is a virtually continuous patchwork of pasture and cultivation: beans, sorghum, bananas, coffee, tea, and tree plantations of eucalyptus and pine.[4] Crops stretch from lot line to lot line; every square inch of land is seemingly accounted for.

Waves of deforestation have accompanied each ethnic upheaval, following the displacement of populations from their previously held lands into as-yet uncultivated, marginal, or "protected" landscapes.[5] Until the 1990 civil war, the government did a decent job of protecting the last remaining forests, all of them inside the three protected forest reserves. During the civil war years, internally displaced Rwandans hid in the protected national forests and cut trees for firewood, while soldiers moved through forests hunting animals for food and cutting trees for building materials. Following the genocide in 1994, it was returning exiles who cleared trees in the national parks, settled, and started farming, while the new government looked the other way at encroachment of protected forest land. Close to a million refugees who had fled the genocide to neighboring countries—along with tens of thousands of Tutsi exiles who had fled earlier eruptions of ethnic violence and had been living abroad—returned to Rwanda in the several years following 1994 looking for farmland and a new life under the newly victorious Rwandan Patriotic Front regime.

In some cases, the UN and the new regime actively encouraged the returnees by officially opening up tracts of formerly protected forest to settlement. With the steep hillsides cleared and the roots that held the soil in place gone, the deforested mountain landscape predictably experienced erosion and landslides. The compounding effects cascaded into a large-scale economic disaster: in the years that followed, the erosion dumped precious soil into the river, caused decreasing fertility of the farm plots, undermined and washed out critical mountain roads, and clogged up the machinery at downstream hydroelectric stations with mud and silt resulting in increased maintenance costs and power outages.[6] Because so much of Rwanda's agriculture takes place on steeply sloping land, up to 40% of cultivated land is considered at risk of severe erosion. All told, about two-thirds of the Akagera National Park and almost all of the Gishwati National Forest Reserve were destroyed by resettlement.

Across Rwanda today, beside the continually terraced hills and nonstop farmland, one notices dense monocultural plantations of young eucalyptus covering small parcels, or lining the roadways in neat alleés. They are the result of attempts to encourage trees as cash crops to fight deforestation; the trees along the roadways are productive placeholders on public rights-of-way. In 2000, the new government under Paul Kagame instituted an annual National Tree Planting Week in which the government provides millions of seedlings for planting by villages and local organizations as part of a coordinated national effort.[7] It has also revived a monthly civic effort known as Umuganda,[8] a compulsory civic holiday on the last Saturday of every month in which all able-bodied adults are expected to help with civic improvement such as wetland restoration, road and small dam construction, erosion control work like terracing, and tree planting and pruning. Together, the National Tree Planting Week and the Umuganda planting efforts, along with annual seedling handouts to farmers, have resulted in extensive increases in Rwanda's forest cover and its plantation areas over the last 15 years, with the government now proposing a goal of 30% forest cover by 2020.[9] During the 2013 National Tree Planting Week, just as an example, the government prepared 32 million seedlings for planting on 37,000 acres,[10] a scale of afforestation that puts the many Million Trees programs in the United States to shame.

The afforestation efforts can be seen both as a reaction to the massive soil erosion that followed the latest wave of deforestation, as well as a collective civic project intended to channel the entire populace into building something new together – something that can grow a national identity that is neither Tutsi nor Hutu, but rather simply Rwandan. Trees, in this case, are employed as active agents in the ongoing shaping of the country's identity, both culturally and politically – as a tool of public education and reconciliation, and as a symbol of the new government's enlightened and responsible governance.

Less noticeable at first, but perhaps more notable, are some specific trees scattered about the agricultural fields in the dryer southern lowlands of Bugesera – older trees, predating the genocide.[11] These trees, of the species *Ficus thonningii*, are known locally as *umuvumu* trees, and they mark the location of households, where they were commonly planted at the time the house was built. In traditional construction, live *umuvumu* trees would be incorporated along with reeds or branches to make the fence around a homestead.[12] With passing generations, larger farms were subdivided among children: each child built their own household, and planted their own *umuvumu* tree. To the visitor, the bright green countryside appears worked, lush, and beautiful. But to many Rwandans, the fence trees standing there without houses next to them must speak of emptiness, of loss in the landscape.

In Bugesera, the hottest, driest, and poorest region of Rwanda, which saw some of the worst killing, one of the first acts to take place during the 100 days of genocide was the burning of houses. The organizers must have known that in carrying out the killing, there would be a lot of ground to cover, and that many people would try to hide and escape. So on the day that the killing began, Hutu youth militias burned down the houses of many Tutsi families – to terrorize them and drive them to gather together in the places of refuge that had served to protect them during previous bouts of ethnic violence in 1959, 1963, and 1973. The tactic was successful: 5,000 people were killed at the church in Ntarama where they had gathered for safety; 10,000 people were killed in and around the church in Nyamata. This pattern was repeated around the country.

The burning of houses also had another intended effect: to make the work of the killers disappear.[13] But if the killers' goal was to achieve invisibility of the preexisting Tutsi population, why then didn't the militias cut down the trees? There is certainly precedent in other conflicts

for the destruction of trees considered to be cultural symbols. In the ongoing war over the perception of legitimate control in Israel and Palestine, Israel and the Jewish National Fund plant pine forests to secure Israeli claims while Palestinian farmers plant olive trees to signify Palestinian ownership;[14] Israel routinely bulldozes olive groves, and Palestinians have used arson to destroy pine plantations in an attempt to fight back against these territorial claims.[15]

In Bugesera, as in many other parts of Rwanda, Hutu families have moved onto the farms that had previously been Tutsi homesteads. But surprisingly, they too have not cut down the *umuvumus*, despite their acute need for firewood and the constant reminder of the previous occupants that the trees present. Since the genocide, it is said that people in Bugasera don't plant *umuvumus* anymore.[16] But somehow those old *ficus* trees still stand amid now-peaceful fields, evoking the memory of murdered families in the Rwandan imagination where others now farm, silently bearing witness to a disappeared population.

Perhaps they still survive because *umuvumu* trees carry another kind of significance for Rwandans. In the pre-colonial period, *umuvumu* trees were associated with the king's dwelling. Planted as a hedge, *umuvumu ficus* trees formed the enclosure of the king's compound, surrounding a small sacred grove.[17] Once the king died and the camp was abandoned, the enclosure's *umuvumu* trees were allowed to continue growing as commemorative groves, not to be utilized by others as fields or pastures, and certainly not to be cut down. Instead they were given the title of *ibigabiro*, or 'authorities,' to be revered as symbols of the old political power on the landscape, with some in time becoming sacred.[18] Treated very differently from naturally occurring forests, various planted vestiges of important homesteads became venerated and preserved. While not as old or as significant, could it be that Bugesera's *umuvumus*, by simply being markers of inhabitation on the landscape, elicit an echo of similar respect? Or is it in the act of recalling the missing, murdered families that the trees assume importance? Philip Gourevitch quotes a Tutsi survivor of the genocide who has resolved to live side-by-side with the murderers of his relatives: "It's our obligation [to coexist], and it's our only way to survive, and I do it every day, and I still can't comprehend it."[19] Similarly, for the families that have taken over the land from those whose houses once stood there, the trees are not so much symbols of atonement, but symbols of their countrymen's victimization: a reality that they must live with every day. If, for the beneficiaries and heirs of the emptied landscape, tyranny lies in the memory of the past and its collective guilt, then the way forward lies in preserving the memory of what was done in Rwanda, so that each day is a promise of "never again" and a renewed obligation of coexistence.

1 As Philip Gourevitch writes, "it was the most efficient mass killing since the atomic bombing of Hiroshima and Nagasaki," *We Wish to Inform You That Tomorrow We Will Be Killed with Our Families: Stories from Rwanda* (New York: Picador, 1998), 3.

2 Tara Mitchell, "International Conflict and the Environment: Case Name: Rwanda and Conflict, ICE Case Study # 23," *Trade and Environment Database* (Spring 1997), http://www1.american.edu/ted/ice/rwanda.htm.

3 Scott Grosse, *More People, More Trouble: Population Growth and Agricultural Changes in Rwanda*, (Washington, DC: USAID Bureau of Africa, September 1994), 23.

4 Elsa M. Ordway, "Political Shifts and Changing Forests: Effects of armed conflict on forest conservation in Rwanda," *Global Ecology and Conservation* 3 (2015): 451.

5 Ibid, 457.

6 Stephanie Hanes, "Loss of Trees, Loss of Livelihood," *The Baltimore Sun* (May 21, 2006) http://pulitzercenter.org/articles/loss-trees-loss-livelihood.

7 Jean Nduwamungu, "Forest plantations and woodlots in Rwanda," *African Forest Forum Working Paper Series*, Vol. 1, No. 14 (2011): 12.

8 *Umuganda* means "coming together with common purpose."

9 Nduwamungu, "Forest plantations and woodlots in Rwanda," 6.

10 "Rwanda to launch the Tree Planting and Afforestation Season 2013–14," Republic of Rwanda Ministry of Natural Resources, http://www.minirena.gov.rw/index.php?id=168&tx_ttnews%5Btt_news%5D=247&cHash=c5e-b58c -d33a0c3e9a2b-cbb04f18477b4 (accessed April 15, 2015)

11 In Bugesera, the oldest *umuvumu* trees tend to be around 50 years of age, which corresponds to the first wave of arrivals to this part of the country. Bugesera was the recipient of waves of refugees of other previous pogroms that have swept the country starting in 1959.

12 Joseph H. Scherer, "The Ha of Tanganyika." *Anthropos* (1959): 841–904.

13 Gourevitch, *We Wish to Inform You*, 21.

14 Irus Braverman, "'The Tree Is the Enemy Soldier:' A Sociolegal Making of War Landscapes in the Occupied West Bank," *Law & Society Review* 42, no. 3 (2008): 449–82.

15 Ari Elon, Naomi Mara Hyman & Arthur Waskow (eds), *Trees, Earth, and Torah: A Tu b'Shvat Anthology* (Philadelphia: Jewish Publication Society, 2000).

16 Ernest Mutwarasibo, interview with author, Ntarama Genocide Memorial grounds (January 8, 2014).

17 Léonidas Ndoricimpa & Claude Guillet (eds), *L'Arbre-mémoire: Traditions orales du Burundi*, vol. 8. (Paris: Karthala Editions, 1984).

18 Didier Babin (ed.), *Beyond Tropical Deforestation: From tropical deforestation to forest cover dynamics and forest development* (Paris: Editions Quae, 2004), 158.

19 Philip Gourevitch, "The Life After," *The New Yorker* 85, no. 12 (2009): 36–49.

STILL LIFE

Refugee camps isolate millions of people worldwide in a legal limbo, corroding refugees' sense of self. Not only are refugees physically displaced from their homes, fleeing from persecution or war, but they are also removed from economic, academic, and political systems that structure communities, sustain social ties, and create meaning in life. Socially constructed identities must be re-assembled in physical and social environments often stripped of life and hope. Most camps bar refugees from earning an income, and it's not uncommon for children to be out of school for years. Higher education is usually not an option, and while informal agrarian and skilled labor jobs can sometimes be found in or near the camp, jobs requiring higher levels of education are scant.

This series of stills is taken from a short clip filmed at an Islamic-funded informal refugee settlement in the Beqaa Valley of Lebanon. The camp was established in 2013 for Syrians displaced by the ongoing civil war in that country. In protracted refugee situations, such as this, refugees will spend an average of 17 years in a camp. While the years accumulate and residents grow, marry, and bear children in the camps, there is little knowledge of how long they will need to remain in this "intractable state of limbo" or whether they will ever return home.

Source: United Nations High Commissioner for Refugees [UNHCR], *The State of the World's Refugees* [UNHCR: Geneva, 2007], 109.

The growing humanitarian crises in recent years throughout the Middle East have focused global media attention on refugee camps.[1] The often seemingly chaotic nature of these camps is highlighted by images of refuse, self-built shelters, and warren-like pathways redolent of shantytowns.[2] An alternate set of images, no less emotionally loaded, are of camps depicted as quasi-military installations, with tents or shelters in long, hierarchically organized rows.[3] But what is often missing from these images is the wider context showing how these 'designed' camp environments become adapted by their inhabitants to include a complexity of ad hoc adaptation and infill. This is in large part because the United Nations (UN) and other humanitarian organizations lack the ability to say what actually constitutes a good camp in the first place. For those organizations, the definition of a camp is simply the minimal list of shelters and other structures installed by them. The existing design guidelines created by these organizations neglect to take into account the rapidly evolving landscapes built upon the camp by the inhabitants themselves, and the complex economies and social networks which expand into these landscapes. By failing to recognize the evolving nature of refugee camps—often eventually developing into the most part of the camp environment—the humanitarian organizations cannot ensure that developments are the best for the camp population as a whole.

Refugee camps, at least those constructed from scratch by the UN or other humanitarian organizations, are planned following global design standards which give guidance for placement of major elements—not just shelter plots, but also schools, health clinics, administrative buildings, and sports areas—down to the exact meter measurement.[4] But within a few months of accepting refugees, most camps bear little resemblance to the initial design and installation. Although the guidance given by humanitarian organizations is precise in dimensions, the types of structures being built (or augmented) and the activities taking place in the camps' spaces are often rapidly transformed by the occupants in ways that move the settlement away from notions of temporary 'camps,' into the more-permanent dimensions of an 'emergency city.'

The major problem is that the guidance documents developed by the United Nations High Commission for Refugees (UNHCR) and other humanitarian organizations[5] were intended for short-term installations, built out of non-permanent materials. For the most part, these guidelines assume that what is produced will remain static in form, as a living snapshot of the camp from the day it was initially installed. It is true that the first camps built according to the current design guidelines in the early 1970s were constructed not in response to refugee movement due to armed conflict, but to population displacement following natural disasters. In such cases there was a realistic expectation that the camps would indeed be temporary and that the inhabitants would be able to move to new housing within a relatively short period of time.[6] In part, the assumed temporary nature of refugee camps can be traced to the history of refugee movements, as well as protection and treatment of refugees, since the 1960s. Until the end of the 1970s, a number of African countries had policies to encourage the permanent settlement of refugees within their countries as part of economic and rural development programs,

Jim Kennedy is a shelter and reconstruction professional, with more than 10 years working for NGOs, the Red Cross, and the UN in shelter programs in response to natural disasters or armed conflicts. Kennedy worked in the Kurdistan region of Iraq between 2013 and 2015 managing and coordinating shelter projects, including projects for upgrading shelters for families with disabilities in Domiz camp and other camps in Kurdistan. He holds a Master of Architecture in Human Settlements and a PhD in Architecture.

✛ INTERNATIONAL RELATIONS, HUMAN RIGHTS, PLANNING

JIM KENNEDY
EMERGENCY LANDSCAPES

and this hospitality towards refugees was enshrined in the African Union's 1969 Convention on Refugees.[8] However, by the mid-1980s, the increasing number of refugees and the protracted nature of conflicts creating the refugee movements, had led to a sense of fatigue amongst many of the host countries. UNHCR responded by declaring, in 1985, that voluntary repatriation, rather than permanent settlement in a host country, was the preferred "durable solution" for all refugees.[7] It appears this ongoing policy has meant that there is little political will to revisit camp design guidelines in a way that would acknowledge that refugees in fact remain in camps for a considerable length of time. This is despite the fact that there continue to be significant numbers of refugees living in "protracted situations" of five years or more, and in the face of camps in northern Kenya (that have existed for almost 25 years)[8] and in Palestine (in existence since 1948).

Camps do not need to exist for very long before changes are spontaneously made by the inhabitants. Experience in camps from Pakistan to the Democratic Republic of Congo, has shown that new arrivals in the camps will start to build barriers and boundaries to their shelter plots immediately after arrival, and that the first stalls selling food and other household items will appear in the camp within two days. The first 'unofficial' pathways or roads, created through the traffic of feet, start to appear within the first month or two. All this is made possible by the fact that the material of the camps is so malleable and plastic in nature: camps are for the most part built in mud. And, despite recent examples from Turkey and Jordan of camps where every shelter is a prefabricated container-like structure surrounded by paving, for most camps around the world, the individual shelters (and many of the self-built shops, mosques, and churches) are also constructed out of mud or other equally malleable natural materials. Given the rapidity with which these changes happen, the often bare-bones administration found in most incipient camps is not in a position to oppose such changes, bar those that would actually impair the functioning of the camp itself.

As each camp evolves and changes through myriad reactions between the specific histories of the inhabitants, as well as the location and environment of the camp itself, the camp takes on an individuality, despite the fact that all camps constructed by UNHCR or other humanitarian organizations are built from the same global design guidelines. In the face of this evolved individuality, it is surprising that there is no definition of what actually makes a good camp among the guidance and review literature produced by UNHCR or other humanitarian organizations.

Adapting research by Tzonis and Lefaivre on the development of non-emergency settlements, I have approached this issue by examining the relationship between the morphology, operations, and performance (M-O-P) of settlements in the context of refugee camps.[9] This concept is usually assumed to be a *linear*, non-repetitive operation, with morphology (the combined shape and space of all elements of the built environment) influencing operations (the ways in which people use those spaces, move through them, or act within them), which then results in a final qualitative assessment of performance (that is, ultimately, answering the question: is the location a good place or not?). The assessment of the performance, in this model, is based upon an observation of a single linear progression (from M to O, and then to P) with the implied assumption that any response to an assessment of the performance would only rest in the mandate and the capacities of the designated authorities. In the case of refugee camps though, the extreme degree to which the materials that constitute the camp are plastic or 'soft-lined' in nature, means that the M-O-P loses its singular, linear aspect. And the performance of the camp is the effective catalyst for the way in which the morphology then continuously changes, as the refugee inhabitants of the camp create new spaces and new structures through the accumulation of the movement through and the usage of a plastic environment. Compelling and supporting all of these changes, is the economic development of the camp, and the evolution of the settlement over time, from an emergency camp to a city.

A recent example of this can be found in Domiz Camp – the largest refugee camp for Syrian refugees in Kurdistan, northern Iraq. With a current population of more than 45,000, Domiz started in March 2013 as a collection of tents initially housing fewer than 15,000 people.[10] In the years since, it has developed to the point where many of the shelters have been rebuilt using concrete blocks, there are shops in the camp selling high-cost items such as washing machines and wedding dresses, as well as shops typical to urban areas in the Middle-East, such as corner bakeries producing bread and local pizza variants. A UN-sponsored supermarket opened in January 2015 and the UN and local government have taken an active role in providing necessary infrastructure such as water and electricity supply, but otherwise most construction has been done spontaneously by the refugees themselves.

Domiz was planned according to UNHCR guidelines, the one significant adaptation at the point of initial planning being that the grid of the UNHCR camp plan followed the grid layout of the local Kurdish municipal urban planning authorities. The dimensions of the individual shelter plots in Domiz are therefore subdivisions of the larger standard housing plots found in the local municipal plans. During 2014, some of the key roads within the camp were paved by local authorities and the selection of the roads given this treatment also conformed largely to the local zoning plans. These matrices of infrastructure and roads, as well as the administrative buildings for the government and for the UN, are the sum of all the 'hard-lined' elements in the camp. Although the installation of the water infrastructure and the surfacing of key roads have been incremental, the initial planning was substantially there from day one.

But, beyond these large-scale armatures the fabric of the camp has changed enormously since its inception. Spaces have become appropriated and enclosed by the expansion of private shelter space, and by the commercial structures installed by the refugees themselves, whilst at the same time, increased erosion of surface drainage channels, and the digging of diversion channels has resulted in increased barriers to accessibility for those with disabilities living in the camp, and has heightened the private/public divide not envisaged as part of the original, open-plan layout of the camp.

The plasticity of the camp, combined with the lack of foresight by the original planners regarding possible changes in both economy and morphology, has meant that the camp now hosts a widening gap between the 'haves' and 'have-nots' in the refugee community. Broadly speaking, those with the greatest personal capital, or the sharpest elbows, are not only able to construct cement-block walls for their shelters (which have effectively become permanent houses in the process), but are also able to construct walls around their entire shelter plots, from the same durable materials. These walls create narrow alleyways between plots and divert surface drainage into the plots of others. In some of the most egregious cases they appropriate, or alternatively block access to, areas intended as public or shared spaces. Whilst the predominant reason for the construction of these exterior walls is undoubtedly to enhance privacy and exert control over personal space (something which is perhaps lacking in other parts of the refugees' lives), another practical reason is to counteract the creation of impromptu paths between shelter plots which, through soil erosion caused by the constant footfalls, have become a source of flooding of adjoining plots during rainy weather.

Using the adapted M-O-P conceptual framework outlined above, the cycle of change in this scenario could be described thus: a morphology of a simple, 'wide-scale' armature is imposed into a very malleable landscape, then, almost instantaneously, a complex of operations occurs that were not anticipated by the original design. While individually undertaken, these operations cumulatively affect the fabric of the camp as a whole, albeit never enough to change the original overarching frame of infrastructure. The assessment of 'performance' available to the outside observer or researcher, comes only occasionally and at periods not directly related to the actual activities in the camp itself; for example, via periodical UN papers or media reports. Meanwhile, on the ground, each individual decision to take a different route from shelter to market or school eventually results in a camp that performs differently in the eyes of the occupants and the plasticity of the camp allows for instantaneous re-assessment by them. They change their activities as an expression of their assessment, which in turn changes the actual fabric, or morphology, of the camp, in a never-ending set of cycles.

However, these myriad and incremental changes should not be seen as being completely randomized or lacking any overall form or direction. In Domiz, there have been points where a groundswell of small operations or actions (such as forging informal pathways between shelter plots), have caused widespread changes in the morphology, such as a rapid increase in the number of families choosing to build concrete-block walls around their shelter plots or the installation of shops in front of shelters, narrowing the pathways, slowing down or diverting the vehicles of NGOs and creating a de facto pedestrian shopping zone. And then suddenly there is an evolutionary jump – from a camp that has shops, to a camp that has shopping zones.

Whilst this adaptation of the M-O-P conceptual framework can help indicate what the inhabitants of the camp see as being a *better* camp, or a better morphology of a camp, or an appropriate physical corrective to some of the stresses of the camp, it still does not provide clear guidance on what is a *good* camp. In particular, the analysis cannot provide complete guidance for how governmental or UN actors should intervene (if at all) to correct growing divisions between those in camps who do and do not have the resources to react to the evolving performance (or spatiality) of the camp in the free-for-all ways described above. What this analytical framework can do, is to provide the evidence necessary for managing the construction, expansion, and upgrading of a camp as part of an integrated approach to not only what is effectively the urban planning and urban design of the camp as an emergency city, but also to economic strategy, educational policy, and what becomes essentially municipal management, in all aspects.

Landscape architects and urban designers may find an emerging role in this process of observation, prediction, and intervention. There are tools from landscape design research, which explicitly take into account the inherently soft-lined, 'organic' nature in which landscapes, planted environments, and local human movements evolve within and through spaces. Studies can be made as to how these tools may be integrated into the current palette of design and assessment tools used in practical circumstances within camps. In addition, there is another set of design tools and a design vocabulary used particularly in the field of urban design, which assume at their core that any activity will be an *intervention*, and will take place in a site where there already are complex human activities and a complex landscape, rather than assuming that everything will be constructed in just one phase, on a tabula rasa. There may be value in constructively contrasting the language and concepts of these sorts of design assumptions, with those of the UNHCR guidelines described earlier in this paper.

And finally, the design disciplines can bring to the discussion experience in working with communities in a consultative environment to inform incremental, cumulative, and mosaic approaches. Such experience would be helpful to ensuring that public spaces remain accessible to the whole community despite inequalities in personal resources, even in the malleable surroundings of a refugee camp.

1 According to the 1951 United Nations Convention on Refugees, a refugee is someone who has crossed an international border because of a well-founded fear of threat or persecution. For the purposes of this paper, "refugee camp" refers to camps planned and constructed not only for refugees, but also for those who have been internally displaced within a country, as well as similar camps, based upon the same guidelines, for those who have lost their housing due to natural disaster.

2 BBC News, "In Pictures: Inside Sri Lanka's vast refugee camp," http://news.bbc.co.uk/2/hi/south_asia/8297760.stm [accessed April 2015].

3 Mac McLelland, "How to Build a Perfect Refugee Camp," *New York Times Magazine* http://www.nytimes.com/2014/02/16/magazine/how-to-build-a-perfect-refugee-camp.html?_r=0 [accessed April 12, 2015].

4 The standard global designs for the camps are based upon a version of 'sites and services' low-income housing settlement planning from the early 1970s, which in turn inherited certain assumptions about the separation of residential zones from other zones, and the separation of functions of spaces, from other schools of urban design from earlier in the 20th century: James Kennedy, *Structures for the Displaced: Service and Identity in Refugee Settlements*, unpublished PhD thesis [Delft: TU Delft, 2008].

5 The major examples of these are *The Sphere Project* [2011], *The Camp Management Toolkit* [2008], and *Transitional Settlements: Displaced Populations* [2004].

6 Ian Davis, *Shelter After Disaster* [Oxford: Oxford Polytechnic Press, 1978].

7 UNHCR, *Durable solutions* [Geneva: UNHCR, 1985]; James Kennedy, *Structures for the Displaced: Service and Identity in Refugee Settlements*, ibid.

8 Kennedy, ibid.

9 Kennedy, ibid; Alexander Tzonis, *Hermes and the Golden Thinking Machine* [Cambridge, MIT Press, 2014].

10 UNHCR, "Thousands of Syrian Refugees Arrive in Iraq, Many with Special Needs" [2012], http://www.unhcr.org.uk/news-and-views/news-list/news-detail/article/thousands-of-syrian-refugees-arrive-in-iraq-many-with-special-needs.html [accessed April 12, 2015].

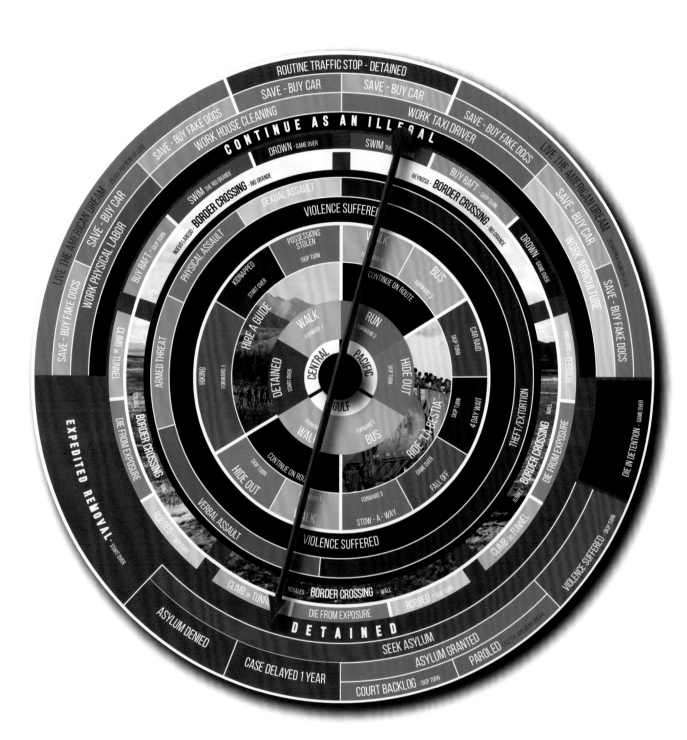

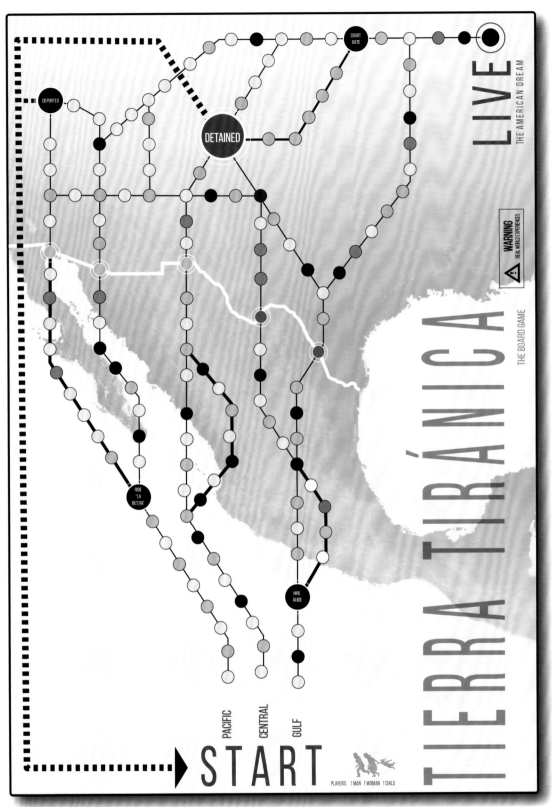

TIERRA TIRÁNICA
THE BOARD GAME

LIVE
THE AMERICAN DREAM

WARNING
REAL WORLD EXPERIENCES

START
PLAYERS: 1 MAN 1 WOMAN 1 CHILD

PACIFIC
CENTRAL
GULF

DEPORTED

DETAINED

COURT DATE

RIDE "LA BESTIA"

HIRE GUIDE

Sources: Exodus, "Crossing Mexico," www.exodus.msf.org/en/mexico.html; Immigration Policy Center, "Mexican and Central American Asylum and Credible Fear Claims: Background and Context," www.immigrationpolicy.org/special-reports/mexican-and-central-american-asylum-and-credible-fear-claims-background-and-context; J. Kasperkevic, "Meet Six Illegal Immigrants Living In The USA," *Business Insider* [April 26, 2012].

Casey Lance Brown works as the Director of Research for P-REX at MIT. Current projects include forecasting of urbanization and technologically enhanced mobility trends for Toyota Research Institute and effects of securitization along borderlands supported by the Charles Eliot Traveling Fellowship. Brown is also a Fellow of the American Academy in Rome and is currently establishing a carbon neutral research base in southern Appalachia.

✛ PLANNING, POLITICS, HUMAN RIGHTS

CASEY LANCE BROWN
THE RISE OF STATELESS SPACE

Distinct shifts in state affairs can be difficult to discern except in hindsight. Consider the Border Patrol Strategic Plan for 1994. It seemed like a typically anodyne bureaucratic plan as far as planning documents go. Illegal immigration in border cities in Texas and California had prompted the new plan due to public uproar over images of galloping groups of undocumented migrants flooding the roads and bridges. With little fanfare, this document laid out a shift in US Border Patrol strategy that would ramify across the entire 2,000-mile-long border with Mexico for decades.

In lieu of a border-wide approach, the plan opted for the targeted disruption of human and drug smuggling routes near urbanized areas (respectively titled Operation Hold the Line and Operation Gatekeeper). The increased presence of fencing and personnel would wither these well-worn smuggling corridors and force the activity into "more hostile terrain, less suited for crossing and more suited for enforcement."[1] The Border Patrol imagined that the parched, rugged terrain of the desert southwest itself would deter and expel most would-be crossers. With this simple phrase, border management evolved from a remote and perfunctory set of policing actions by a bare-bones agency into a set of complex spatial strategies, counter-measures, and unintended consequences of military scale.

The Border Patrol strategy was deadly effective in shifting activity to the desert. Unfortunately, the supposed suppressant turned out to be more of a remote beacon. Within a few years, the tentacles of the smuggling operations probed new, more dangerous routes through the remote deserts of the southwest. By 2000, the Tucson sector alone racked up 616,000 apprehensions, an 870% increase from 1992.[2] This sector includes portions of the Sonoran and Chihuahuan deserts – large and treacherous swaths of territory where only extreme adaptations allow survival.

Previous: Patrol roads have multiplied in recent years throughout the public lands of the southwest.

Top: Rocky outcrops provide prospect over the vast uninhabited stretches of southern Arizona.

Opposite: Desert scrub and *arroyos* (dry creek beds) provide cover and sanctuary for both illegal immigrants and migrating predators.

These same remote, wild desert zones that draw adventurous tourists offer difficult-to-monitor sanctuaries for smugglers and their human traffic. The observed rise in migrant deaths—near 500 per year and largely resulting from exposure to heat or cold—is a primary indicator of the lack of state presence.[3] The bodies and belongings sit in an unclaimed limbo much like the terrain that claimed their lives. With only periodic presence of the patrols and an officially, or unofficially, deterred public, some of these zones have become quasi-stateless.

Forming Extra-National Space

Though no maps will document any change in status, the threat of danger and marginally successful surveillance have precipitated pockets of absence where the rule of law is questionable. In this ambiguous space, smugglers and patrollers reign supreme, decoying their movements and becoming unwitting executioners when leaving migrants alone to traverse the inhospitable terrain. In these isolated areas, a Fed-Ex van, aerial drone, or oilfield service truck might not be what it seems.

Arising from the mix of heightened crossing activity and the post-9/11 call for securitization, the US embarked on the most extensive shuffling of governmental agencies since the beginning of the Cold War. The consequence for the border region was the repetitive deployment of National Guard units, 9,000 new patrol agents, a ten-drone aerial regiment, and hundreds of aircraft and mobile detection units along 700 miles of new fencing. The Border Patrol air units now form the largest civilian law enforcement air force worldwide.[4]

This amplified patrolling footprint, combined with the increasingly violent drug trade along the border, triggered the formation of extra-national territory. In these contested spatial zones, the normal laws and standards of protection no longer apply. Border

sections of previously open public land in wildlife refuges and national parks are now closed indefinitely to avoid endangering the visiting public. Even where the closure is not officially declared, the persistent stopping and questioning by the highly active Border Patrol shatters the tranquility of a recreational excursion. The trash and detritus left by night watches, laydowns (temporary waiting areas used by immigrants to avoid detection), and dendritic trails left by immigrant movements mar the otherwise protected land. Patrol roads scar the slow-to-repair desert floor. The network of immigrant footpaths near the remote smuggling outposts spread invasive seeds and compact soils in fragile, protected zones. Organ Pipe Cactus National Monument accumulated 2,553 illegal roads and trails in recent years that spider out into the wildest sections.[5]

Apex predators could benefit from a vacated, stateless zone, but only in the absence of manmade obstructions. The fence blocks migrating and venturesome mammals, such as jaguars.[6] New fencing along the Texas border could diminish or extinguish the last remaining populations of ocelot and the thorny scrub that houses them. Helicopter patrols add intense noise pollution that blankets previously silent desert tracts, potentially stressing the already endangered populations of Sonoran pronghorn. These impacts propagate from an ineffective, reactive style of immigration law enforcement that fails to take into account the land's protective environmental status. The REAL ID Act of 2005 permits these ecological damages via a sweeping authority that waives any laws that may impede border fence construction. As a consequence, extensive border spaces have become extra-national with respect to environmental protection as well.

Globalizing Statelessness

Border regions are undergoing transformations in various global hotspots as economic disparity and political gamesmanship push and pull on their spatial integrity. For example, Ceuta and

1 US Customs and Border Protection, "Border Patrol Strategic Plan: 1994 and Beyond," *1994 Border Patrol Strategic Plan – Prevention Through Deterrence*, US Border Patrol (July 1994), 1–14.

2 US Department of Homeland Security, Office of Immigration Statistics, *Yearbook of Immigration Statistics: 2004* (2006), http://www.dhs.gov/yearbook-immigration-statistics (accessed January 29, 2015).

3 US Government Accountability Office, *Illegal Immigration: Border-Crossing Deaths Have Doubled Since 1995; Border Patrol's Efforts to Prevent Deaths Have Not Been Fully Evaluated*, GAO-06-770 (9 August 2006), http://www.gao.gov/new.items/d06770.pdf (accessed December 21, 2014).

4 US Customs and Border Protection, "Air and Marine Forces: A Rich and Varied History of Service," http://www.cbp.gov/border-security/air-sea/about/history (accessed January 29, 2015).

5 National Park Service, "Sonoran Desert I&M Network (SODN)," http://science.nature.nps.gov/im/units/sodn/parks/orpi.cfm#PedFence (accessed February 13, 2015).

6 Susan Greenberg, "Jaguars Win Critical Habitat in US," *Nature News*, http://www.nature.com/news/jaguars-win-critical-habitat-in-us-1.11255 (accessed February 12, 2015).

7 Milène Larsson, "Storming Spain's Razor-Wire Fence: Europe or Die," *Vice News*, https://news.vice.com/video/storming-spains-razor-wire-fence-europe-or-die (accessed January 26, 2015).

8 Eyal Weisman, "Lethal Theory," *Log* 7 (Winter/Spring 2006): 53–77.

9 Carlos Ramos-Mrosovsky, "International Law's Unhelpful Role in the Senkaku Islands," *University of Pennsylvania Journal of International Law* 29 (2014): 903–46.

Top: The expansion of patrol roads and illegal tracks have fragmented the semi-arid grasslands and provided new conduits for invasive seed dispersal.

Opposite: This former ranch and wildlife preserve has sustained heavy foot traffic and environmental damage due to shifting immigration and enforcement tactics, forcing closure of its border section.

Melilla, Spain's remnant colonial enclaves on the northern coast of Morocco, occupy a strategic position that is not lost on the multitude of amnesty-seeking migrants from West, Central, and North Africa. Technically, the legal process begins the second migrants touch EU soil, instantly switching status from illegal immigrant to potentially legal asylum seeker. This principle of immigration law has become a major animating force behind the creation of new stateless spaces.

Much like in the US, Spain's national police (*Guardia Civil*) greatly enhanced both its physical presence and legal latitude in these territories. A simple, remote border became the epicenter of illegal crossing activity, prompting the erection of a triple-layer fence that was met with an explosion of counter-measures by immigrants to gain entry. As a deterrent, Spain and Morocco created an extra zone between the layers of fencing that may or may not be officially Spanish (and thus EU) territory. Taking advantage of the spatial ambiguity, agencies have contracted with hired police on the Moroccan side to forcibly block the immigrants before they cross and to swiftly deport the few that reach the stateless zone between the fences.[7]

The question remains whether the immigration turmoil in these corridors will escalate to the level of the perpetual Israeli-Palestinian conflict, probably the most extreme example of contested border space. There, an "inverse geometry" reigns, where Israeli Defense soldiers move "through walls" and see the constructed space itself as the "very medium" in which they have total freedom to operate.[8] This saturated enforcement forms almost an inversion of the concept of a separation border. Lobes of Israeli settlements and their associated defense walls greatly expand the Palestinian border, engulfing and segregating new territories. Are these border bulges and contained lobes Israeli land or Palestinian territory?

As the developed world's economic wealth expanded, so did the draw to enter that economic sphere from the less-developed world. Wherever this disparity collides spatially, new fissures appear in the form of fences, no-go zones, and legal limbos like the Korean Demilitarized Zone (DMZ). These spreading fissures push the definition of surrounding borderlands from remote, often accessible public land to tangled zones of police power and abandonment, where background legal protections may be suspended and all activity is intensively surveilled by drones, optical equipment, and ground sensors. Unintentionally, these surges in enforcement presence often trigger the probing that exposes new access routes through land, water, or air. Consider the ever-simmering row between Japan, China, and Vietnam over scattered islands and subsurface coral reefs such as the Senkaku/Diaoyu Islands southwest of Okinawa, Japan. International oceanic boundaries posed by these semiaquatic land specks will serve as the next frontier of border skirmishes, as international law is too fuzzy to prescribe a solution.[9]

Every troop deployment, immigration policy action, and triple-layer fence re-partitions border space into new, buffered zones of potential statelessness. Previous enforcement actions along the southwestern border of the US have pushed illegal activity toward Texas, where legislators are now debating whether to extend their National Guard deployment. Imagine this constant seesaw between surging immigration and subsequent surges in enforcement slowly levering border space into physical and legal nether-zones. People, animals, and laws are deterred, leaving only statelessness and its unintended consequences – human rights abuses, public land closure, and environmental degradation. Without remedies for the underlying economic disparities that drive the illegal immigration and smuggling conveyor belt, the most likely scenario remains further propagation of statelessness.

Acknowledgements

Original research on the border region for this essay was generously supported by the Charles Eliot Traveling Fellowship, awarded by the Landscape Architecture Department in the Harvard University Graduate School of Design.

AT THE EDGE OF SOVEREIGNTY

Although these landscapes appear as if they are artificially spliced together, they in fact depict borders between nations. What is evident in these images are the ways in which different policies, economic conditions, and cultural practices can create radically different landscape forms and land-use patterns on either side of a national border. Each image shows how—just by virtue of an arbitrary line—one unified place with the same geological and ecological conditions can become two different worlds.

Sources: Aerial view of Bolivia–Brazil border, © Google. Map data © CNES/Spot Image (2015). Aerial view of USA–Mexico border, © Google. Map data © US Geological Survey (2012). Aerial view of South A... Country gross domestic product (GDP)/per capita, Central Intelligence Agency, *The World Factbook* (2014).

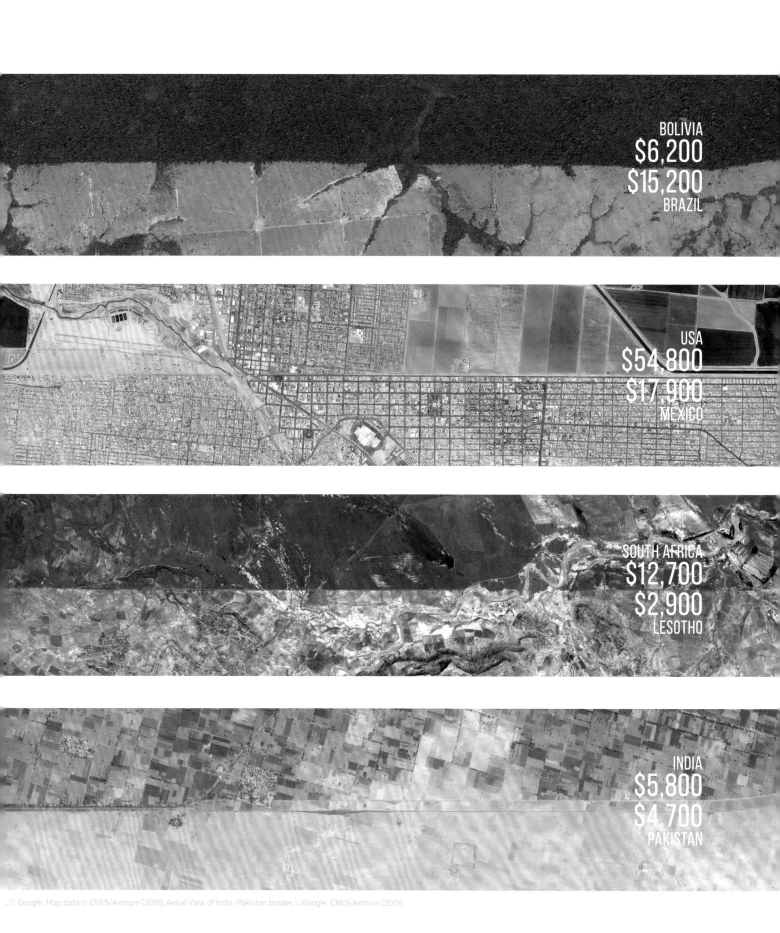

BOLIVIA
$6,200
$15,200
BRAZIL

USA
$54,800
$17,900
MEXICO

SOUTH AFRICA
$12,700
$2,900
LESOTHO

INDIA
$5,800
$4,700
PAKISTAN

ARCHITECTURE AND ARMED CONFLICT

Nick McClintock is completing a Masters of Landscape Architecture and Masters of Architecture at the University of Pennsylvania School of Design. He holds a Bachelor of Arts from Middlebury College.

✛ ARCHITECTURE, URBAN STUDIES, HISTORY

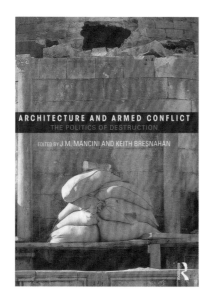

J.M. Mancini and Keith Bresnahan introduce *Architecture and Armed Conflict: The Politics of Destruction* as a broadening of the conversation about architectural destruction beyond the preoccupation with World War II in the literature to date. By recruiting their authors from history, anthropology, and archaeology, as well as architectural history and preservation, the editors frame destruction as an act and instrument of cultural production. Sitting, as the editors claim, at the intersections of disciplinary boundaries, the chapters raise questions about the contradictory representation of destruction and the sometimes-tenuous links between the act and its later portrayal. Arranged in five parts covering contemporary conflicts, representations of architectural destruction in ancient and early modern contexts, the role of iconoclasm, the fate of architecture in post-conflict zones, and the reconstruction or redevelopment of ruins, *Architecture and Armed Conflict* captures a wide swath of both time and space.

In her chapter examining Berlin's Gedächtniskirche (literally, Memory Church), Kathleen James-Chakraborty captures the tension and contradiction between layers of accumulated meaning. She discusses how the Gedächtniskirche became the locus of a debate about German national identity and the legacy of National Socialism. What began as "a patriotic icon became...a symbol of principled resistance, of wartime destruction and victimhood, of religion's resistance to capitalism, and, finally, of capitalist democracy,"[1] all of which pulled at the meaning of redevelopment on the site in unexpected ways. The particular acuity with which the objects and places of architectural destruction shift in meaning is a central theme of the volume.

In Bresnahan's chapter on the destruction and subsequent re-incarnations of the infamous Bastille prison in Paris these shifts in meaning become simultaneously and separately productive.[2] Bresnahan demonstrates how the destruction of the Bastille was leveraged by revolutionaries simultaneously to profit from and mythologize the revolution. Among the many examples he cites is a set of Bastille miniatures, carved from bricks of the destroyed prison, that were gifted to the capital cities of France's 83 newly formed *départements* (a municipal level of government administration). Such a process demonstrated the power of the destruction-relic to connect and mediate between individual experience and collective political identity.[3] The fact that Pierre-François Palloy, the man behind the production of the miniatures, was coincidently activist and entrepreneur—the bricks were but one of several profit-making ventures he generated from the legacy of the Bastille—makes the larger question of productive destruction more ideologically fraught.

While the Bastille's destroyers manipulated destruction to create a new social order, in Jyoti Pandey Sharma's chapter "Disciplining Delhi: The 1857 Uprising and Remodeling of the Urban Landscape," a similar reformist ideology becomes entwined with a program of demolition for repressive colonial interests. Sharma argues that the British Crown's tenuous grip on power after a protracted uprising in Delhi led to retaliations against the indigenous population, recast as the need to combat disease with urban clearance. In the post-uprising political climate, troop movement, land seizure, and demonization of particular religious and ethnic groups became conveniently entwined with public health campaigns, infrastructure development, new zoning, and other spurious tools of colonial rationalization and 'progress.' Sharma makes a convincing case that this rationalization was based as much on fear and Orientalist attitudes of 'otherness' as on any genuinely progressive agenda. Ironically, these 'improvements' have now become the focus of contemporary preservation and heritage efforts.

In a bid to examine how destruction at the hands of empire creates new cultural mandates among those actually subjected to it, anthropologist Christina Schwenkel's "Architecture and Dwelling in the War of Destruction in Vietnam" focuses on the northern city of Vinh, which endured protracted bombing in the late 1960s. Her examination of the architecture that emerged within and around Vinh during the war in response to the bombing seeks to understand how an indigenous population dwells amidst a war of destruction.[4] Schwenkel argues that dwelling in Vinh became defined as a constant state of 'mobility' between home and protection, or work and protection, and an eventual blurring of the lines between production, protection, and movement. This at first took the form of networks of tunnels that became progressively used as dwelling spaces as local Vietnamese were forced into them more and more frequently. When the intensity of the bombing became too great, the urban population was forced to evacuate the city and re-establish factories, banks, clinics, schools, and every other facet of public life in the forest. Despite this relocation, families periodically returned to the city when the danger subsided, only to be forced back to the countryside when the B-52s reappeared. By examining the effect of destruction across multiple scales of both time and space, Schwenkel expands destruction and its cultural meaning to sites far from the craters themselves.

Loosely pulled together under the five sections laid out at the beginning of this review, the diversity of sites and analytical methods represented in *Architecture and Armed Conflict* makes for an eclectic package of essays that might have benefited from a clearer curatorial agenda. In particular, there is no attempt made by the editors to synthesize the collection or provide insights as to what conclusions can be drawn for the discipline of architecture (or indeed, landscape architecture). For instance, the parallels between the deliberate sowing of salt to poison conquered Assyrian land[5] and the use of Agent Orange as a defoliant in the Vietnam War could have yielded a theorization of the nature and history of landscape-warfare. Equally, the colonial legacy of destruction as a tool for control and progress could have been examined by reference to Rita Harkin's chapter on the destruction of historical Belfast for speculative housing development in the wake of the Good Friday agreements,[6] and Sharma's chapter on the clearance of Delhi in the name of a healthier, more 'modern' city. These thematic threads remain latent, and a conclusion that draws out the connections across chapters–the conflation of ideology and representation, the contradictions in the use of destruction for construction of a political identity, and the effects of destruction on cultural adaptation–seems a missed editorial opportunity. Nevertheless, *Architecture and Armed Conflict* does open numerous avenues for analyzing and interpreting architectural destruction in a heretofore understudied context.

1 Kathleen James-Chakraborty, "The Use of Ruins in Post-war German Church Reconstruction," in Keith Bresnahan & J.M. Mancini (eds), *Architecture and Armed Conflict: The Politics of Destruction* (New York: Routledge, 2015), 201.

2 Keith Bresnahan, "Remaking the Bastille: Architectural Destruction and Revolutionary Consciousness in France, 1789–94," in ibid., 59.

3 Ibid., 64.

4 Christina Schwenkel, "Architecture and Dwelling in the 'War of Destruction' in Vietnam," in ibid., 17.

5 Heather D. Baker, "'I Burnt, Razed (and) Destroyed Those Cities': The Assyrian Accounts of Deliberate Architectural Destruction," in ibid., 45–57.

6 Rita Harkin, "Anything Goes: Architectural Destruction in Northern Ireland After 'The Troubles,'" in ibid., 147–164.

JoAnne Mancini and Keith Bresnahan (eds), Architecture and Armed Conflict: The Politics of Destruction (New York: Routledge, 2015), 220 pages, Paperback, RRP $53.95.

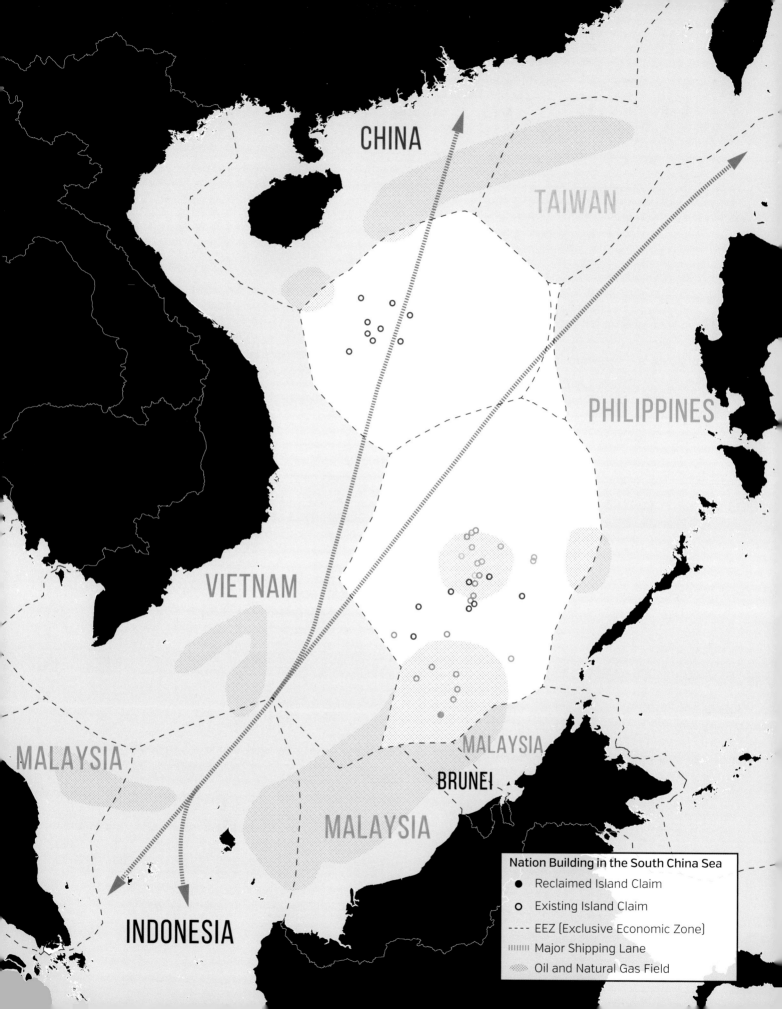

CHINA

TAIWAN

VIETNAM

PHILIPPINES

MALAYSIA

MALAYSIA

BRUNEI

MALAYSIA

INDONESIA

Nation Building in the South China Sea

● Reclaimed Island Claim

○ Existing Island Claim

- - - - EEZ (Exclusive Economic Zone)

||||||| Major Shipping Lane

▦ Oil and Natural Gas Field

NATION BUILDING

The United Nations Convention on the Law of the Sea was signed into international law in December 1982. Among other things, the Convention established Exclusive Economic Zones (EEZ), which give nations the right to exploit natural resources within 200 nautical miles of the coastal baseline. Nowhere is there more at stake than in the oil-rich shipping lanes of the South China Sea where nations are competing for sovereignty through the spurious practice of constructing islands from which to cast their claims. While an island's landmass might measure a mere acre, a successful claim grants the claimant state exclusive rights to fish and to exploit offshore oil and gas within the EEZ. If there is no island, build one.

Step 1

Locate a reef/outcrop in disputed or international waters near a shipping route, fishing area, or oil/gas resources.

Step 2

Build initial structure on reef and place colonizer to hold claim as a habitable structure.

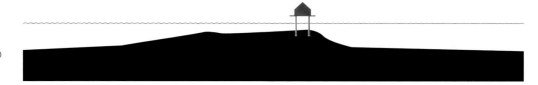

Step 3

Dredge channel for ship access and pile spoils to create an artificial island on top of the reef/outcrop.

Step 4

Build a concrete plant, seawall, helipad, landing strip, and other structures as necessary.

Step 5

Await UN resolution or self-proclaim the EEZ. Extract resources, regulate shipping, and "leave before the sea rises."

200 m EEZ (Exclusive Economic Zone)

Sources: http://www.economist.com/news/asia/21645268-unprecedented-building-boom-reclamation-marks?fsrc=rss%7Casi; http://in.reuters.com/article/2015/04/15/southchinasea-philippines-usa-idINKBN0N616L20150415; http://www.marineregions.org/; http://www.southchinasea.org/files/2011/08/Overlapping-EEZ-Claims-and-Oil-Fields.png; http://www.janes.com/article/43935/castles-made-of-sand-chinese-land-reclamation-in-the-south-china-sea.

CHRISTOPHER MARCINKOSKI

THE TYRANNY OF
SPECULATIVE URBANISM

Christopher Marcinkoski is an Assistant Professor of Landscape Architecture and Urban Design at the University of Pennsylvania. He is a licensed architect and founding director of PORT, a leading-edge urban design consultancy. Previously he was a senior associate at James Corner Field Operations in New York where he led the office's large-scale planning and urban design work. He is the author of *The City That Never Was* (2015).

+ ECONOMICS, REAL ESTATE, URBAN DESIGN, REGIONAL PLANNING

The term tyranny often conjures up images of hegemonic dictators, religious ideologues, human rights violations, or militant activists. Urbanization, on the other hand, is rarely seen through such a pejorative lens, let alone considered something tyrannical. Yes, there are often concerns about population displacement and potential environmental disturbances. But for most politicians, planners, economists, and designers, urbanization activities are seen as a kind of panacea – the essential solution to even the most intractable of issues. In this context, while historically most expansions of settlement and infrastructure have ultimately served to produce a relatively positive outcome in the long term, an increasing number of projects are appearing globally that are motivated less by real demographic or market demands than by political hubris and global economic ambitions.[1] These projects have a far greater likelihood of sustained interruption or failure than urbanization activities that emerge from more conservative motivations and, as such, pose a significant risk of disturbance and unrest for those polities that engage in these activities. I refer to this phenomenon as *speculative urbanization*, and contend that its increasing proliferation should be understood as an urgent social, environmental, and economic concern, as well as an emerging form of tyranny given the growing universality of its pursuit.

For the purposes of this discussion, I have defined speculative urbanization as "the construction of new urban infrastructure or settlement for primarily political or economic purposes, rather than to meet real (as opposed to artificially projected) demographic or market demand."[2] If this definition is expanded slightly, we can include the legislative re-designation and re-parcelization of land for the specific purposes of increasing its monetary value. The phenomenon relates primarily to activities occurring at the periphery of established urban areas, or in entirely exurban contexts where urbanization activities are operating at the scale of a district or territory, rather than at the scale of a single parcel or building.[3]

While examples of speculative expansions of settlement and infrastructure can be found as far back as ancient Rome, the last 15 years have seen the most dramatic and consequential instances of the phenomenon, as well as a clear intensification of its incidence. From the ghost estates of Ireland, to the empty suburbs of the U.S. Sunbelt, to the artificial oases of Dubai, to the white elephant infrastructures of Spain, to the unoccupied new towns throughout western China, these speculative expansions of settlement have proliferated like no other time in history.[4]

Given the economic and social disruption caused by the failure of these recent initiatives, it is worth noting that historically, urbanization activities have tended to follow economic growth. On the occasions when these activities do outpace their corresponding economy, a surplus is created and some sort of market correction is required: price, volume, etc. To an extent, this is exactly what occurred in the U.S. and Ireland, albeit to an irrational extreme. However, this correlation between urbanization activities and economic growth is more and more frequently being inverted. Here, as was the case in Dubai and Spain, urbanization is expressly being undertaken to invite outside investment and generate economic activity regardless of real demand. This often means the pursuit of projects that are wildly over-scaled or inappropriate to the current circumstance of a given context and, as such, result in a high incidence of failure – either through low occupancy, incompletion, or abandonment.

The belief here is that these familiar urbanistic pursuits—high-speed rail, international airports, congress halls, super-tall office buildings, stadiums, museums, high-rise condo towers, luxury suburban housing districts—will provide both a signifier and an instrument of economic and political status for a city or state that will in turn lead to external investment and economic growth for that polity. Urbanization is treated as a kind of empty vessel into which external capital will, in theory, accumulate. As a result, subscription to this belief is increasingly producing a kind of chicken-or-egg question

Opposite: Incomplete speculative dormitory town 60 km northwest of Madrid, Spain.

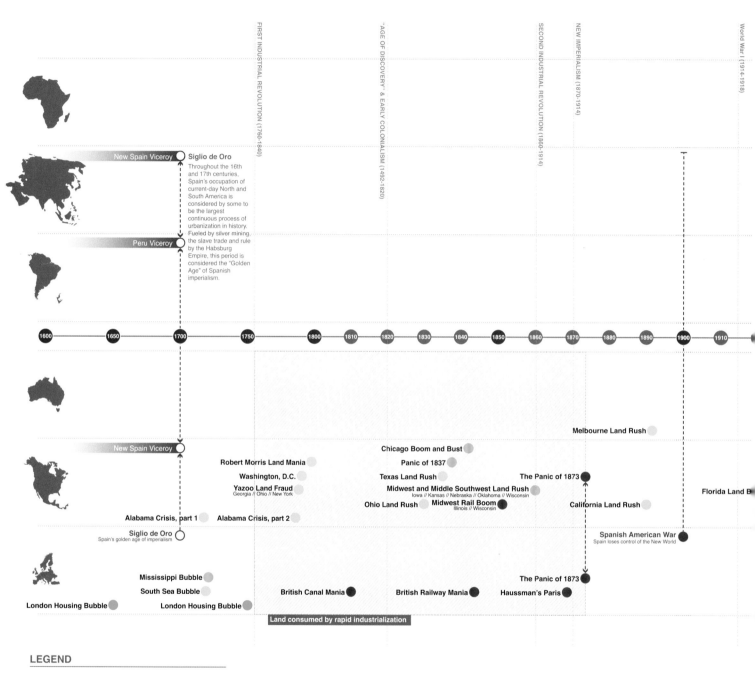

FIRST INDUSTRIAL REVOLUTION (1760-1840)

"AGE OF DISCOVERY" & EARLY COLONIALISM (1492-1820)

SECOND INDUSTRIAL REVOLUTION (1860-1914)

NEW IMPERIALISM (1870-1914)

World War I (1914-1918)

New Spain Viceroy ○ **Siglio de Oro**
Throughout the 16th and 17th centuries, Spain's occupation of current-day North and South America is considered by some to be the largest continuous process of urbanization in history. Fueled by silver mining, the slave trade and rule by the Habsburg Empire, this period is considered the "Golden Age" of Spanish imperialism.

Peru Viceroy ○

1600 — **1650** — **1700** — **1750** — **1800** — **1810** — **1820** — **1830** — **1840** — **1850** — **1860** — **1870** — **1880** — **1890** — **1900** — **1910**

New Spain Viceroy ○

Melbourne Land Rush ●

Chicago Boom and Bust ●

Robert Morris Land Mania ● Panic of 1837 ●

Washington, D.C. ● Texas Land Rush ● The Panic of 1873 ●

Yazoo Land Fraud ● Midwest and Middle Southwest Land Rush ●
Georgia // Ohio // New York Iowa // Kansas // Nebraska // Oklahoma // Wisconsin

Ohio Land Rush ● Midwest Rail Boom ● California Land Rush ● Florida Land B
Illinois // Wisconsin

Alabama Crisis, part 1 ● Alabama Crisis, part 2 ●

Siglio de Oro ○ Spanish American War ●
Spain's golden age of imperialism Spain loses control of the New World

Mississippi Bubble ●

South Sea Bubble ● The Panic of 1873 ●

London Housing Bubble ● British Canal Mania ● British Railway Mania ● Haussman's Paris ●

London Housing Bubble ●

Land consumed by rapid industrialization

LEGEND

● **Land** [e.g. parcels, plots and subdivisions] ⊙→ **Ongoing** [in progress / various colors]

● **Agriculture** [e.g. timber, wheat, and cotton] ▌ **International** [global in effect / various colors]

● **Infrastructure** [e.g. rail, canals and highways] **Geography** [origin of speculative event]

● **Building** [e.g. commercial prop. and housing]

● **Urbanization** [all of the above]

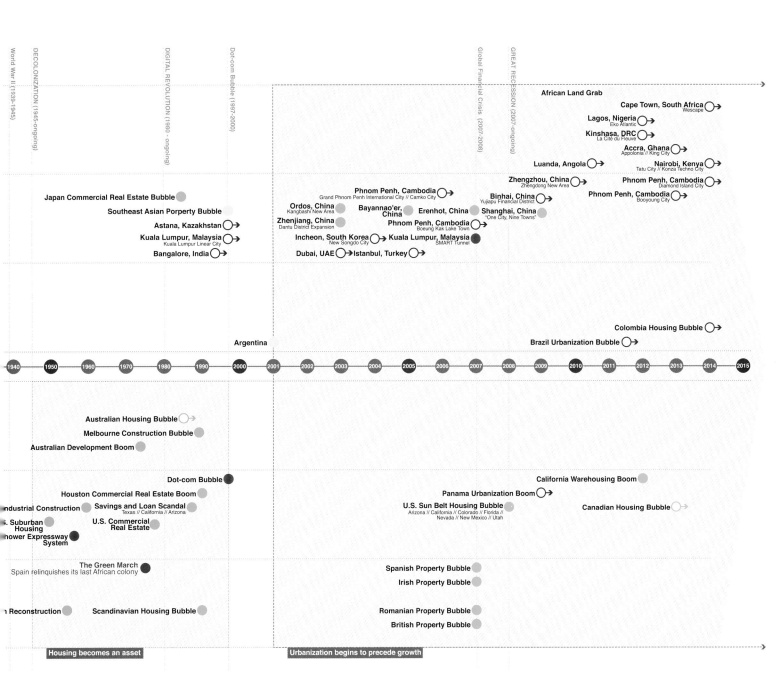

A PARTIAL TIMELINE OF SPECULATIVE URBANISM

Above: Proposals for speculative new cities in sub-Saharan Africa. From top left, clockwise: Eko Energy Estate, Nigeria; Kigramboni City, Tanzania; Appolonia City of Light, Ghana; Hope City, Ghana; Konza Techno City, Kenya; Eko Atlantic, Nigeria.

when it comes to the role urbanization activities are asked to play relative to a city or state economy. Should economic growth dictate the intensity of urbanization activities? Or can the deployment of new infrastructures and settlement successfully serve to drive economic growth over the long term? To understand the potential implications of this paradox, consider for example a particular response of the global real estate system to our most recent financial crisis.

African Urbanization Post-2008

Shortly after the global economy came screeching to a halt in late 2008–and with it, many of the endeavors mentioned above–a new wave of speculative proposals surprisingly began to appear, albeit in a radically different economic, political, geographic, and environmental milieu. What remaining investment capital was still sloshing around globally had shifted focus and found its way into a region where the urgent need for updates to urban infrastructure and settlement could not be disputed: sub-Saharan Africa. In this context, much of what was being proposed was not actually surplus (as was the case in the U.S, Spain, and Ireland) but rather inapt, radically incongruous in scale and scope relative to actual demand. As such, beyond their clear misalignment with the realities of the African milieu, what many of these proposals for new settlement and infrastructure also implied was the threat of further exacerbating deficient urban conditions by shifting severely limited capital resources away from basic necessities in order to fund these speculative endeavors.[5]

Many of the proposals for urbanization that have appeared in this context since the global financial crisis can be characterized as vanity pursuits, motivated by political agendas and economic returns rather than by the realities and demands of the settings into which they were to be deployed.[6] The familiar tropes of 'knowledge,' 'technology,' 'security,' and 'luxury' embellish many of the names of these initiatives, relying on the hyperbolic jargon of global real estate development for their identity. In many cases, mobility infrastructures like high-speed rail, toll highways, or new or expanded international airports companion the introduction of these proposals, encouraging additional speculative building by providing an apparatus around which these activities can accumulate. A group of familiar international funding sources and government-linked companies, alongside recognizable engineering and planning multinationals, appear again and again in much of this work. This similarity between proposals in terms of central actors and proposed outcomes, in even the most divergent of contexts, suggests a universal recipe for urbanization-driven economic growth being peddled indiscriminately across the continent.

Ongoing research undertaken in the School of Design at the University of Pennsylvania has found no fewer than 60 proposals for speculative expansions of settlement introduced or undertaken since 2008 within Africa's 20 largest state economies. That said, examples can be found in many of the continent's smaller economies as well. Each of these cases are a minimum of 50 hectares (approx. 125 acres) in size, and are sited as peripheral expansions of settlement adjacent to existing cities or on exurban greenfield sites. Population and economic growth projections for the continent, in combination with the shoddy state of its older cities, are said to be the motivation behind these initiatives. Yet many of these "African

New Towns" are heavily reliant on models of urbanization-driven economic growth that unapologetically borrow from exogenous models employed in places like China and the Middle East. Problematically, these are models that have a completely different set of material or demographic resources from which to draw, not to mention entirely different governance and land tenure systems. What is particularly noteworthy is that in many of these examples, this speculative development is often instrumentalized for purposes completely unrelated to accommodating actual urbanization demands.

For example, Tatu City, a 2,500-acre residential and industrial park development 20 km north of Nairobi, Kenya is one of at least five speculative developments being pursued throughout sub-Saharan Africa by Rendeavour, a subsidiary of the Moscow-based Renaissance Group – a leading emerging markets investment company.[7] Arnold Meyer, the former CEO of Rendeavour has stated, "the West has peaked in terms of economic growth and the new markets are in Africa," with "the main drivers of this growth [being] cities."[8] In the Democratic Republic of Congo, the proposed La Cité du Fleuve development outside of Kinshasa is being financed by a British hedge fund that has little prior connection to urbanization activities, but is a major investor in African agricultural and mineral resources.[9] In Lagos, Nigeria, the need for protection from sea-level rise and seasonal storm events was leveraged into the creation of a 10 km2 piece of reclaimed land on which a gated luxury district for 250,000 is under construction just a few kilometers away from one of Africa's most notorious informal settlements.[10] Elsewhere, the president of Angola, José Eduardo dos Santos, made the construction of 1,000,000 new homes within four years a central platform of his 2008 reelection campaign.[11] That Kilamaba, the first phase of this initiative, is mostly inaccessible to the average Angolan is immaterial. The point is that the massive landscape of colorful new housing is meant to signify a new, modern Angola.

Obviously, not every example is identical in terms of its motivations, incongruity, or degree of duplicity. However, given the broader political, economic, and environmental disturbances that followed on the various speculative developments of the early 21st century, a critical inquiry into these ongoing endeavors is urgently needed. While this forum is not conducive to an in-depth discussion of multiple examples of these pursuits, two cases in particular are useful in characterizing the increasing tyranny of speculative urbanization across the African continent.

Exerting Influence – China in Angola

The Angolan case mentioned above is perhaps the most familiar example due to its widespread coverage in mainstream media. In 2012, the BBC ran a story titled "Angola's Chinese-Built Ghost Town" which showed for the first time the physical results of President dos Santos' promise of one million homes.[12] The project in question, known as Kilamba Kiaxi, is located roughly 30 km south of the country's capital, Luanda.

1 "Booms and Busts: The beauty of bubbles," *The Economist* (December 18, 2008), http://www.economist.com/node/12792903.

2 Christopher Marcinkoski, *The City That Never Was* (New York: Princeton Architectural Press, 2015), 10.

3 Ibid.

4 For a more complete discussion of these and other historical examples of speculative urbanization, see "A Brief History of Speculative Urbanization" in ibid, 16–48.

5 Vanessa Watson, "African Urban Fantasies: Dreams or Nightmares?," *Environment and Urbanization* 26, no. 215 (2014): 229.

6 While it is true that the initial planning for some of these projects began prior to the 2008 crisis, the proliferation of these types of initiatives following the crash suggests a clear belief in the efficacy of urbanization as an ideal instrument for capturing impatient global capital.

7 See Rendeavour's online portfolio of development initiatives on the African continent, http://rendeavour.com/portfolio/.

8 Anne-Sylvaine Chassany and Simon Clark, "Renaissance Plans Congo City Bigger Than Kenya's $5 Billion Tatu," *Bloomberg Business*, (September 9, 2011), http://www.bloomberg.com/news/articles/2011-09-09/renaissance-plans-congo-city-bigger-than-kenya-s-5-billion-tatu.

9 See Jessica Chu, "Investigation Into German Involvement In Land Grabbing In Zambia," *Zambia Land Alliance and Caritas Zambia* (March 23, 2012), http://www.woek.de/web/cms/upload/pdf/kasa/publikationen/zla_caritas_2012_investigation_into_geman_involvement_in_land_grabbing_in_sambia_choma_dws.pdf and Hawkwood Capital statement on corporate social responsibility: http://www.hawkwoodllp.com/page/97/Corporate-Social-Responsibility.htm.

10 Martin Lukacs, "New, privatized African city heralds climate apartheid," *The Guardian* (January 21, 2014), http://www.theguardian.com/environment/true-north/2014/jan/21/new-privatized-african-city-heralds-climate-apartheid.

11 Yifei Zhang, "Angola's $3.5B, Chinese-Built Ghost Town," *International Business Times* (July 9, 2012), http://www.ibtimes.com/angolas-35b-chinese-built-ghost-town-722923.

12 Louise Redvers, "Angola's Chinese-Built Ghost Town," *BBC* (July 2, 2012), http://www.bbc.com/news/world-africa-18646243.

The BBC article's images of colorful blocks of collective housing spreading out relentlessly across an arid plane were widely disseminated on social media and other news platforms. The intense interest in the story was likely due to the scale of what was built, in combination with its similarities to many of the so-called Chinese ghost towns that were increasingly being covered in western media at the time. That the project also happened to be built by the Chinese state-owned CITIC Group (formerly China International Trust and Investment Corporation) in exchange for access to Angola's massive oil reserves only intensified western curiosity and suspicion.

While the Angolan state press has pushed back on the narrative of Kilamba as a ghost town–as recently as September 2013, claiming that all of the flats were sold–the real story for our purposes is the immensity of the project (roughly 8.25 km2], in combination with the motivations behind its construction.[13] In this context, it should be highlighted that what was shown in these images is roughly one-tenth of what is actually planned for the project. And according to a 2012 report by the China Academy for Urban Planning and Design, Kilamba Kiaxi is but one of five satellite cities proposed for the periphery of Luanda, all to be financed by the Industrial and Commercial Bank of China and built by CITIC. As such, this case epitomizes the phenomenon of speculative urbanization in that it represents a massive piece of urban development motivated not by social provisions or market demand, but by overt political agendas and dubious financing mechanisms.

Exporting Expertise – Singapore in Rwanda

While the Chinese incursion into Angola appears to be driven by larger geopolitical agendas, the case of Singapore in Rwanda seems much more focused on monetizing expertise in urban development and peddling 'proven' models of urbanistic 'success' into new, underserved markets. The project in question is the proposed Kigali 2020, a remade capital city for Rwanda that endeavors to permanently jettison the familiar images of genocide and war by replacing them with the clean, green, hyper-efficiency of "a central African Singapore."[14] Planned and designed by Surbana–a Singapore-based, government-linked company–the sheer ambition, audacity and incongruity of the proposed city is consistent with much of the firm's other planning work in places like Mumbai and Lagos.[15] While not a true parastatal, Surbana trades upon the expertise of having had a central role for more than 50 years in the Singapore story – perhaps the single most successful example of urbanization-driven economic and political transformation in history.

This new vision for Kigali sees the capital as a telecom, finance, and logistics hub for Central Africa. Existing slum areas have been re-envisioned as ecological corridors and bustling business districts replete with hotels, coffee shops, and other cosmopolitan urban amenities. Despite the seeming irrationality of this endeavor, construction of Kigali 2020 was quickly undertaken upon completion of the masterplan in 2008 despite not having secured tenants or investors. Thomas Goodfellow notes in an essay titled "Kigali 2020: the politics of silence in the city of shock" that "slum clearances and expropriations have left enormous scars of turned earth... across the urban landscape...[including] roads, water pipes and even fibre-optic cables," seemingly awaiting the development of future buildings yet to come.[16] Notably, the Rwandan government's pursuit of the Singapore model is not limited to the physical. The country is following Singapore's lead in using social security funds to help finance housing development, and there are even some in the various ministries who believe that in the long run, Rwanda may ultimately become 100 percent urban, a metric that no country in the world other than Singapore actually meets.[17] To say that the proposed urbanization strategy is out of touch with existing circumstances would be an understatement.

It is interesting to note that Singapore's former prime minister Lee Kuan Yew, the architect of the country's rapid ascendance during the second half of the 20th century, cited the dysfunction of former British colonies in Africa during the 1960s as a driving motivation for how he would look to reposition Singapore in the world following independence.[18] That his model of urbanization-driven economic prosperity is now, half a century later, being exported back into this reference context–albeit bypassing the various phases of transformation that have lead to the entrepôt's current global status–is a clear indicator of the widespread belief in the transformative economic and political potential of urbanization activities, regardless of where, how, or for whom they are being deployed.

Implications

As I have argued elsewhere, the proliferation of proposals for speculative settlement and infrastructure has corresponded not only with the increased liberalization of global finance over the last three decades, but also (more notably) with the emergence of city rankings and comparative benchmarking as a quasi-scientific pursuit over the same period.[19] These rankings have emerged from a range of sources including academic institutions, transgovernmental organizations, global management consultancies, and popular media, among others. They are considered to carry varying degrees of weight and credibility, with new rankings continuing to appear regularly.

My interest in the appearance and proliferation of these rankings is twofold. The first is the implication of correlating economic status with physical urban form. Although economic competition between cities is not new, tying a polity's competitiveness directly to the presence of certain urban accoutrements is. This correlation has created a kind of arms race, particularly within developing economies, where speculative building is seen as the means to a particular economic and political end. In this sense, it is worth pointing out that the central actor in many of the African examples mentioned above is linked to a polity that has a demonstrated record of using speculative building to a 'successful' end – Singapore, China, Abu Dhabi, etc.

The second interest is what can be seen as an increasing subscription to these rankings by politicians and their advisors as the basis of defining both economic growth policies and physical planning strategies for a polity. This growing subscription implies the distillation and flattening of urban form down to a set of basic elements that are somehow universally appropriate, regardless of the specificity of a particular context. This is a reductive view of the contemporary city, defined solely by the metrics of economists and the social sciences. It frames urbanization activities in transactional terms, focusing exclusively on the economic potential of the physical products of these activities.

Of course, the pursuit of these recipes is not limited to the examples discussed above. To these, we can easily add ongoing endeavors in Panama, Turkey, Kazakhstan, Qatar, and Vietnam, among many others. As recently as March 2015, a massive new capital city for Egypt was proposed for the outskirts of Cairo in order to "spark a renaissance in the [country's] economy."[20] This new city, planned for five million residents and to be built in five to seven years, is just the latest example of an increasingly prevalent belief in urbanization as the ultimate instrument of 21st-century economic production and global status, particularly for developing economies. In this sense, we might characterize the tyrannical nature of speculative urbanization threefold: one, the increasing universality of subscription to an urban growth model rooted in building and replication regardless of political, geographic, or economic context; two, the prioritization of spectacle over substance when it comes to these large-scale expansions of settlement or infrastructure; and three, the complicity of the urban design disciplines, either as naïve pawns or willing participants, in these activities.

Obviously, my intention here is not to dismiss all large-scale contemporary urbanization initiatives as problematic or unnecessary. However, what is critically important to understand is that given the changing motivations behind these activities, and in turn, their increasing risk of interruption or failure, it is essential that the urban design disciplines central to their production profoundly rethink how they conceive, plan, design, and deploy these initiatives. In doing so, turning an eye toward the elaboration of systems of adjustment and revision over time, rather than rigidly focusing on a preferred or single outcome, should become a central focus of this work.[21] Without such a shift, the social, environmental, and economic consequences of these pursuits will only continue to intensify. Catastrophic failure of these kinds of speculative endeavors has already occurred, with little long-term impact on their pursuit. As such, only by inflecting the products and processes upon which the system relies can design and planning look to confront the tyrannical nature of speculative urbanization.

13 "Kilamba City flats sold out," *Angola Press News Agency* [September 4, 2013], http://www.portalangop.co.ao/angola/en_us/noticias/sociedade/2013/8/36/Kilamba-City-flats-sold-out,9a874ce7-f6fa-4f25-b35a-9d888d4c07d4.html.

14 Thomas Goodfellow, "Kigali 2020: the politics of silence in the city of shock," *Open Democracy* [March 14, 2013], https://www.opendemocracy.net/opensecurity/thomas-goodfellow/kigali-2020-politics-of-silence-in-city-of-shock.

15 While the Denver-based firm Oz Architects did much of the initial planning for Kigali 2020, the current scheme is clearly driven by Surbana given its characteristic disconnect with reality as seen in other projects such as their work in Mumbai. http://www.surbana.com/mumbai-metropolitan-region-concept-plan/

16 Goodfellow, "Kigali 2020."

17 Ibid.

18 Jini Kim Watson, "The Way Ahead: The Politics and Poetics of Singapore's Developmental Landscape" in *The New Asian City: Three-dimensional Fictions of Space and Urban Form* [Minneapolis: University of Minnesota Press, 2011], 179–181.

19 Marcinkoski, "City Rankings and Global City Ambitions" in *The City That Never* Was, 49–51.

20 "Egypt unveils plans to build new capital east of Cairo," *BBC* [March 13, 2015], http://www.bbc.com/news/business-31874886.

21 For a more complete discussion of how design and planning might reorient their approach to speculative urbanization, see "Urbanization Beyond Speculation" in Marcinkoski, *The City That Never Was*, 220–235.

BUILT BY

When the Residence Act of 1790 declared Washington, DC as the location of the first planned US capital, little existed on the "ten miles square" of agricultural land ceded by the (then) slave states of Maryland and Virginia. Located on the Potomac on the furthest inland point navigable by boats, the site chosen by the city's namesake had a population of just over 2,000 ten years after its founding. Far from major population centers and a skilled labor workforce, planners and builders of the capital were faced with a shortage of workers. Thus, the infrastructural and architectural construction relied extensively on skilled enslaved labor to build the capital of the New World.

The US capital developed as both a transportation nexus of the slave trade and a facilitator of enslaved domestic and labor workers from its conception until Lincoln's Emancipation Proclamation in 1863. This history is evidenced in the buildings we now see as icons of freedom and liberty. In almost every stage of construction including quarrying, milling, sawing, bricklaying, and carpentry, enslaved labor was used to build both the Capitol Building and the White House, complementing a smaller workforce of free blacks and whites. Whilst slaves from the capital made up the majority of the labor force, many others were likely hired from farms and households in surrounding areas.

Today, a Congressional Slave Labor Task Force serves to ensure the work of slaves is acknowledged in the capital. So far, the only monument to the slave effort is a marker in Emancipation Hall at the US Capitol Visitor Center. The marker commemorates the role played by the laborers who built the capitol, "including enslaved African Americans."

Sources: William Allen, *History of Slave Laborers in the Construction of the United States Capitol* (Washington, DC: Office of the Architect of the Capital, 2005); Damani Davis, "Slavery and Emancipation in the Nation's Capital," *Prologue Magazine* 42, no. 1 (2010); Jesse Holland, *Black Men Built the Capitol: Discovering African-American History in and around Washington, DC* (Guildford: Globe Pequot, 2007); Joseph Kapsch, "Building Liberty's Capital," *American Visions* 10, no. 1 (1995): 5–13.

DRAWN BY C.R. PARSONS

Massachusetts Av.		Government Printing Office			Stanton Sq.	(NORTH EAST DIV)
U.S. Post Office	City Hall Park	City Hall	Pennsylvania Av.	B.& O.R.R. Depot	THE CAPITOL	
Bureau	Metropolitan Hotel	National Hotel				Navy Yard
Washington Market			B.& P.R.R. Depot	Botanical Garden		
The Mall	Agricultural Dpt. Smithsonian Institute	National Musuem		Jefferson School	(SOUTH EAST DIV)	U.S. Arsenal
Bureau of Engraving & Printing	LONG BRIDGE					EAST BRANCH OF THE POTOMAC

Y OF WASHINGTON.

VIEW FROM THE POTOMAC - LOOKING NORTH.

The complicated project of converting cities from mechanical to ecological systems is surely the primary design challenge of the 21st century. But this does not sanction landscape architecture's current mass-production of images of urban places as miraculously eco-paradisiacal. Just when it seemed we had all agreed that the new nature couldn't look like the old, on Planet Photoshop, 'sweet nature the redeemer' is back. And who can resist? Just as sex has long been used to sell objects, nature now sells cities. Nature sells design and so design sells nature. Everyone wins.

Of course, on Planet Photoshop it's not nature per se that we are talking about – it's landscape scenography for a global theater. With the real city of toxicity and chaos camouflaged from view, the programmed people of Planet Photoshop cavort about in the foreground – invariably delighted by the wetlands and aviaries their masters have made for them. On Planet Photoshop everyone is an eco-tourist, the thermostat is set to 70, and nature doesn't bite. On Planet Photoshop everyone is politically correct but nothing ever changes.

Whilst on the surface, images of Planet Photoshop's eco-paradise seem perfectly innocent and confer virtue on all those involved in their production, they are not so simple. The ecology they advertise is specious and the bliss they promise is, like the original paradise itself, ahistorical and apolitical. By disguising their own mechanical fabrication and papering the city with green muzak, these eco-paradisiacal images aid and abet the evil modernity they otherwise claim to redeem.

With verdant nature smeared all over the lens, eco-paradise anaesthetizes its audience and forecloses the possibility of aesthetic invention and, by extension, the possibility of any sociopolitical actions other than passive observation. Indeed, it is not uncommon for the pretty people of Planet Photoshop to be pictured taking photos of the very landscape they themselves have been flattened into. Uncannily, on Planet Photoshop everyone seems fascinated with the view and yet it all looks more or less the same.

The question, then, is not whether or not to reject the eco-paradisiacal, for surely the ecological and the paradisiacal are landscape architecture's primary referents. The question is whether these can be directed toward an aesthetic that more honestly reflects the technical difficulty and poetic depth of denatured conditions.

Richard Weller is Chair of Landscape Architecture at the University of Pennsylvania and the Martin and Margy Meyerson Chair of Urbanism.

+ DESIGN CRITICISM

MORE BIRDS + BUTTERFLIES!

RICHARD WELLER

THE INNOCENT IMAGE

ADD DOLPHIN(S)?

AMS

IMAGE CREDITS

Trees and Memory in Rwanda

p. 78: Collage by, and courtesy of, Hannah Davis with component images "Photographs of Genocide Victims at the Genocide Memorial Centre in Kigali, Rwanda" by Adam Jones, used under CC BY-SA 3.0 license via Wikipedia Commons and "Umuvumu Tree" by, and courtesy of, Nicholas Pevzner.

p. 80–81: Collage by, and courtesy of, Hannah Davis with component images "A Eucalyptus Plantation in Final Stages at Arimalam" by Balaji Kasirajan, used under CC BY-SA 3.0 license via Wikipedia Commons and "Eucalyptus Trees Blooming," public domain.

Still Life

p. 82–83: Images by, and courtesy of, Helen Yu.

Emergency Landscapes

p. 84–89: Images by Carlo Gheradi, courtesy of Jim Kennedy (images desaturated).

Tierra Tiránica

p. 90–91: Images by, and courtesy of, Hannah Davis.

The Rise of Stateless Space

p. 92–97: Images by, and courtesy of, Casey Lance Brown.

At the Edge of Sovereignty

p. 98–99: Images © Google with map data as attributed in situ.

Book Review: Architecture and Armed Conflict

p. 100: Architecture and Armed Conflict: The Politics of Destruction (New York: Routledge, 2015) by JoAnne Mancini and Keith Bresnahan (eds).

Nation Building

p. 102–103: Images by, and courtesy of, Nate Wooten.

The Tyranny of Speculative Urbanism

p. 104: "Speculative town 60 km northwest of Madrid, Spain" by, and courtesy of, Christopher Marcinkoski.

p. 106–107: "A partial timeline of speculative urbanization" by, and courtesy of, Christopher Marcinkoski.

p. 108: "Appolonia City of Light, Accra, Ghana" by Reandevour; "Eko Energy Estate, Lagos, Nigeria" by MZ Architects; "Konza Techno City, Konza, Kenya" by Konza Technopolis Development Authority; "Eko Atlantic, Lagos, Nigeria" by Eko Atlantic, "Hope City, Akkra, Ghana" by RLG Communications; "Kigamboni New City, Dar es Salaam, Tanzania" by Kigamboni Development Agency, all courtesy of Christopher Marcinkoski.

Built by Slaves

p. 112–113: "The City of Washington Birds-Eye View from the Potomac Looking North" (1892) by Currier & Ives, New York, public domain (color overlay).

The Innocent Image

p. 114–115: Image by, and courtesy of, Dan Ke and Hannah Davis.

Upcoming Issues

p. 118 "Map of Science derived from Clickstream Data" by Bollen J, Van de Sompel H, Hagberg A, Bettencourt L, Chute R, et al. (2009) "Clickstream Data Yields High-Resolution Maps of Science", PLoS ONE 4(3): e4803. doi: 10.1371/journal.pone.0004803, used under CC BY license.

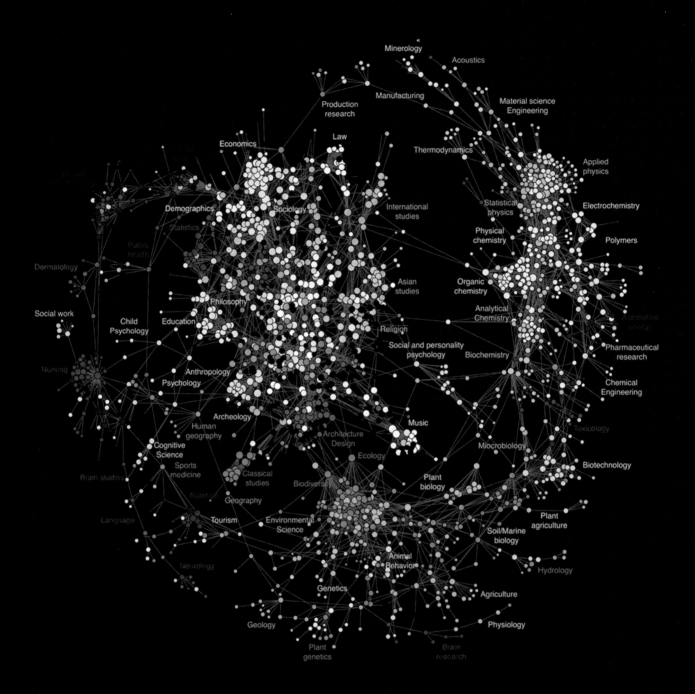

Minerology

Acoustics

Production
research

Manufacturing

Material science
Engineering

Economics

Law

Thermodynamics

Applied
physics

Demographics

Sociology

International
studies

Statistical
physics

Electrochemistry

Statistics

Physical
chemistry

Polymers

Public
health

Asian
studies

Organic
chemistry

Dermatology

Social work

Philosophy

Religion

Analytical
Chemistry

Alternative
energy

Child
Psychology

Education

Social and personality
psychology

Biochemistry

Pharmaceutical
research

Nursing

Anthropology

Chemical
Engineering

Psychology

Archeology

Music

Toxicology

Human
geography

Architecture
Design

Miocrobiology

Cognitive
Science

Ecology

Biotechnology

Sports
medicine

Classical
studies

Plant
biology

Brain studies

Biodiversi

Plant
agriculture

Nutrition

Geography

Soil/Marine
biology

Language

Tourism

Environmental
Science

Hydrology

Neurology

Animal
Behavior

Agriculture

Genetics

Physiology

Geology

Plant
genetics

Brain
research

WILD SPRING 2015

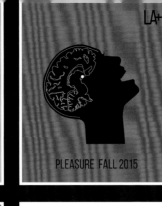

PLEASURE FALL 2015

TYRANNY SPRING 2016

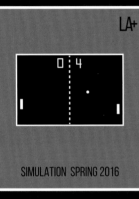

SIMULATION SPRING 2016

INTERDISCIPLINARY JOURNAL
OF LANDSCAPE ARCHITECTURE

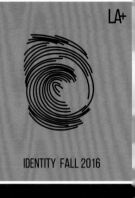

IDENTITY FALL 2016

UPCOMING ISSUES

LA+ [Landscape Architecture Plus] from the University of Pennsylvania School of Design
is the first truly interdisciplinary journal of landscape architecture. Within its pages
you will hear not only from designers, but also from historians, artists, philosophers,
psychologists, geographers, sociologists, planners, scientists, and others. Our aim is
to reveal connections and build collaborations between landscape architecture and
other disciplines by exploring each issue's theme from multiple perspectives.

LA+ brings you a rich collection of contemporary thinkers and designers in two issues
each year. To subscribe follow the links at WWW.LAPLUSJOURNAL.COM